Cambridge Elements

Elements in Ancient East Asia
PEOPLE: Family, Gender, Class and the Individual
edited by
Erica Fox Brindley
Pennsylvania State University
Rowan Kimon Flad
Harvard University

UNEARTHING FLUCTUATING WEALTH INEQUALITY

Household Disparities at Jōmon and Yayoi Sites in Southern Kantō, Japan

Yoko Nishimura
Gettysburg College

Shaftesbury Road, Cambridge CB2 8EA, United Kingdom

One Liberty Plaza, 20th Floor, New York, NY 10006, USA

477 Williamstown Road, Port Melbourne, VIC 3207, Australia

314–321, 3rd Floor, Plot 3, Splendor Forum, Jasola District Centre,
New Delhi – 110025, India

Cambridge University Press is part of Cambridge University Press & Assessment,
a department of the University of Cambridge.

We share the University's mission to contribute to society through the pursuit of
education, learning and research at the highest international levels of excellence.

www.cambridge.org
Information on this title: www.cambridge.org/9781009644273

DOI: 10.1017/9781009406901

© Yoko Nishimura 2026

This publication is in copyright. Subject to statutory exception and to the provisions
of relevant collective licensing agreements, no reproduction of any part may take
place without the written permission of Cambridge University Press & Assessment.

When citing this work, please include a reference to the DOI 10.1017/9781009406901

First published 2026

A catalogue record for this publication is available from the British Library

*A Cataloging-in-Publication data record for this Element is available from the Library
of Congress*

ISBN 978-1-009-64427-3 Hardback
ISBN 978-1-009-40692-5 Paperback
ISSN 2632-7325 (online)
ISSN 2632-7317 (print)

Additional resources for this publication at www.cambridge.org/Nishimura

Cambridge University Press & Assessment has no responsibility for the persistence
or accuracy of URLs for external or third-party internet websites referred to in this
publication and does not guarantee that any content on such websites is, or will remain,
accurate or appropriate.

For EU product safety concerns, contact us at Calle de José Abascal, 56, 1°, 28003
Madrid, Spain, or email eugpsr@cambridge.org

Unearthing Fluctuating Wealth Inequality

Household Disparities at Jōmon and Yayoi Sites in Southern Kantō, Japan

Elements in Ancient East Asia

DOI: 10.1017/9781009406901
First published online: March 2026

Yoko Nishimura
Gettysburg College
Author for correspondence: Yoko Nishimura, ynishimu@gettysburg.edu

Abstract: This Element examines how archaeology can contribute to the investigation of ancient wealth disparities, using the Jōmon and Yayoi periods in Japan as a case study. It analyzes 1,150 pit dwellings from 29 archaeological sites in southern Kantō, dating from the Late Jōmon to the end of the Yayoi period (ca. 2540 BC–AD 250). Household wealth is estimated through pit dwelling floor area, with Gini coefficients calculated for each site. Results show relatively low inequality in the Late Jōmon, a slight decline in the Middle Yayoi, and a marked rise in the Late Yayoi period. Notably, average floor area decreased in the Late Yayoi period. These patterns raise broader questions about how wealth disparities were shaped by communal norms, settlement organization, the rise of agriculture, and expanding trade networks involving iron tools. This research underscores archaeology's unique ability to illuminate long-term economic transformations.

Keywords: inequality, material wealth, Jomon, Yayoi, Japan

© Yoko Nishimura 2026

ISBNs: 9781009644273 (HB), 9781009406925 (PB), 9781009406901 (OC)
ISSNs: 2632-7325 (online), 2632-7317 (print)

Contents

	Introduction	1
1	Socio-Economic Inequality in the Jōmon Period	2
2	Socio-Economic Inequality in the Yayoi Period	4
3	Archaeological Perspectives on Economic Inequality	6
4	Measuring Material Wealth in Archaeology	9
5	Issues with Quantification of Material Wealth	15
6	The Study Area in the Southern Kantō Region	19
7	Data	23
8	Results	26
9	Discussion	30
	References	38

An Online Appendix for this Element is available at www.cambridge.org/Nishimura

Introduction

In contemporary society, widening wealth disparity shows no sign of abating and is a significant social issue. Archaeology excels in providing insights into historical topics, including the development of economic inequality by incorporating long-term data spanning hundreds or thousands of years. Price and Feinman (2010: 2) define inequality as "the organizing principle of hierarchical structure in human society . . . manifested in unequal access to goods, information, decision making, and power." Inequality takes many forms and typically denotes vertical stratifications in social, political, religious, and economic dimensions. Disparities in power, status, and prestige can be considered social inequalities, while differences in wealth are primarily economic inequalities. These different inequalities are often intertwined, creating a positive feedback loop between them. Numerous archaeological studies have extensively addressed the evolution and mechanisms of various inequalities in ancient societies across the globe (e.g., Ames 2007; Flannery and Marcus 2012; Mattison et al. 2016; Mittnik et al. 2019; Price and Feinman 1995, 2010; Smith 2021).

When investigating inequality, it is crucial to differentiate the development of persistent or institutionalized inequality that is passed down through generations from more ephemeral cases. Mattison et al. (2016: 185) define persistent institutionalized inequality as "differential access to power or resources involving the institutionalization of status hierarchies through hereditary privileges or positions such as social classes, castes, hereditary titles, or inheritable differences in wealth." Bowles et al. (2010: 8) similarly assert that economic and social inequality is generally assessed by the extent of enduring ascribed differences among individuals or families in access to valued goods, services, or status, and by the transmission of these advantages across generations.

Disparity of wealth is closely linked to economic inequality, as economic inequality refers to the unequal distribution of wealth and income among individuals or groups within a society. Killewald et al. (2017: 380) distinguish wealth as the total accumulation of a household's assets and resources, subtracting the value of debts, from income, which refers to the inflow of financial resources at a specific point in time. Archaeologists typically define wealth as the sum of desirable or valuable assets and goods, both social and material, existing at the individual, household, or community level (e.g., Schneider 1974: 256). Unequal access to valued goods, services, and status is consequently linked to the uneven distribution of wealth. Wealth, including land, housing, and livestock, generates income and other benefits for individuals and families (Bogaard et al. 2019: 1130).

This study uses the Jōmon 縄文 and Yayoi 弥生 periods in Japan as a case study to examine how archaeology can effectively investigate ancient wealth

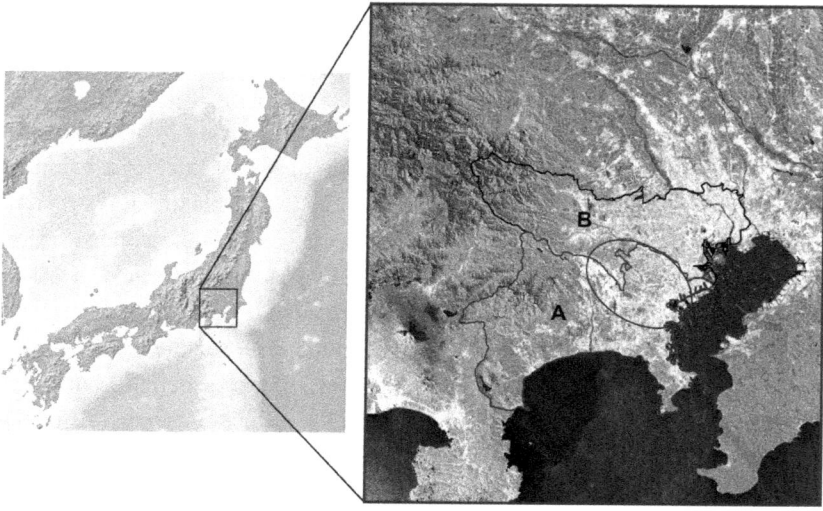

Figure 1 Map of Japan highlighting the area of investigation in the southern Kantō region. (A) Kanagawa Prefecture, (B) Tōkyō Metropolis. Base maps: right by NASA; left by GrandEscogriffe (CC BY-SA 4.0, via Wikimedia Commons). Maps were cropped and modified by the author (lines and labels added).

disparities by drawing on its methodological strengths. It examines the development of wealth inequality by analyzing a large sample of pit dwellings excavated from several dozen archaeological sites across southern Kantō 関東, dating from the Late Jōmon to the end of the Yayoi period (ca. 2540 BC to AD 250) (Figure 1) (see Kobayashi et al. (2020) for Kantō periodization). The floor area of each dwelling serves as a proxy for household wealth, and Gini coefficients were calculated for each site to assess the degree of inequality. The results show that the relatively low level of wealth disparity in the Late Jōmon period slightly declined during the Middle Yayoi period, followed by a significant rise in inequality in the Late Yayoi period. The Late Yayoi period also saw a substantial decrease in the average size of pit dwellings. These patterns suggest that the fluctuating levels of wealth inequality during these periods may have been linked to major transformations, including communal regulations, shifts in settlement structure, the spread of agriculture, and the rise of iron-based trade networks.

1 Socio-Economic Inequality in the Jōmon Period

Many Jōmon communities, especially after the Late Jōmon period, are considered complex hunter-gatherer societies. Despite the absence of fully developed agriculture and social stratification, many communities were sedentary and engaged in rich ritual activities and long-distance trade. For a long time, Jōmon society was believed to be egalitarian and devoid of social stratification. This perception was partially influenced by the economic limitations of a hunter-gatherer lifestyle, such as insufficient surplus and storage.

The ongoing debate over whether a permanently unequal or stratified society existed during the Jōmon period is known as the Jōmon Stratified Society Theory. This discussion began in the late 1980s and gained prominence in the early 2000s (Yamada 2020: 29–31; Yamamoto 2005). Within the framework of this theory, social stratification has been defined in various ways. For example, Sasaki 佐々木 (2002: 34) defines it as a prestige-based hierarchy grounded in social and economic disparities resulting from the division of labor and the accumulation of surplus. Drawing on burial data and ethnographic accounts of hunter-gatherer societies, particularly those in resource-rich environments, scholars have argued that complex hierarchical communities had already emerged during the Jōmon period (Anzai 2006; Kobayashi 2000: 112–114; Nakamura 1999; Pearson 2007; Sakaguchi 2011; Sasaki 2002; Watanabe 1990). For instance, Sakaguchi 坂口 (2011) investigates status differentiation through mortuary variability at the Kiusu キウス and Bibi-4 美々4 sites in Hokkaidō 北海道. During the Late Jōmon period, elite graves located within the *shūteibo* 周堤墓, a communal burial mound enclosed by a circular embankment, contrast clearly with non-elite graves outside the *shūteibo* in terms of grave goods and markers. Sakaguchi's findings reveal variability both in the number of corporate groups and in the relative power dynamics between sites. As a methodological approach, Japanese archaeology has predominantly relied on burial data to assess wealth disparity in settlements from the Jōmon and Yayoi periods. These studies provide important insights into the complexity and potential stratification of social structures in Jōmon society; however, the theory has not been conclusively proven.

Scholars who oppose the Jōmon Stratified Society Theory argue that Jōmon society was in the process of transitioning towards stratification in a complex manner. These scholars propose that it was either not yet stratified or was at a stage of becoming stratified, transitioning into a transegalitarian society (Ames 2007; Hayashi 2001; Kaneko 2005; Shitara 2022; Takahashi 2001). Shitara 設楽 (2022: 167) argues that Jōmon society reflects the beginnings of a stratified society in a transegalitarian manner, characterized by a heterarchical rather than a strictly hierarchical structure. Ames (2007) also argues that there is no clear evidence of strong inequality or political stratification (e.g., settlement hierarchy) during this era, describing the Jōmon culture as transegalitarian (lacking stratification). Kaneko 金子 (2005)

examines the burial practices of the Kamegaoka 亀ヶ岡 culture, a Late Jōmon period culture primarily in the Tōhoku 東北 region, and concludes that it may be unreasonable to seek evidence of a stratified society in the graves of the Kamegaoka culture.

2 Socio-Economic Inequality in the Yayoi Period

Around the end of the tenth century BC, large groups of people began migrating from the Korean Peninsula to the Japanese archipelago, bringing with them technologies such as rice agriculture and metallurgy from neighboring regions of the Asian continent. These innovations gradually spread throughout Japan, leading to significant societal and lifestyle changes during the Yayoi period (Crawford 2011; Miyamoto 2018).

The Wei Zhi's 魏志 account of the Wa 倭 people, compiled by the Chinese historian Chen Shou 陳寿 during the late third century as part of the "*Records of the Three Kingdoms*," suggests the existence of a hierarchical society during the Yayoi period, but it does not specify when this hierarchical society began in Japan. Regarding the social hierarchy of the Yayoi period, Wei Zhi's account mentions the existence of three classes: the ruling class, commoner class, and slave class in late third-century Japan (Saeki 2018). From the descriptions in the Wei Zhi, it can be inferred that within the ruling class, there were additional differences in status. At the highest rank were the supreme rulers, such as queens and kings, below whom were positions such as officials and deputies held by individuals who oversaw administrative functions. In addition, the Wei Zhi also mentions that this period is believed to have seen widespread warfare across the Japanese archipelago during the latter half of the second century.

In Japanese archaeology, the existence of social inequality during the Yayoi period has been primarily discussed from the perspective of the emergence of chiefs and chiefdom societies. Regarding economic inequality, measuring wealth disparities by the quality and quantity of grave goods is still mainstream. Although the expansion of the chieftain class and the accompanying widening of wealth disparities tend to be considered together, we must keep in mind the possibility that there is a temporal gap between these two factors. Matsugi 松木 (1996: 254) exemplifies this by stating that, in the northern Kyūshū 九州 region, a chieftain system had been established at least by the Middle Yayoi period. On the other hand, based on the burial systems and settlement conditions, wealth disparities between the chieftain class and ordinary members within the group are not observed until the Kofun 古墳 period.

Social inequality and stratification during the Yayoi period are argued to have emerged earlier in northern Kyūshū and the Kinki 近畿 region compared to the

Kantō region. Negita 禰宜田 (2019: 263) asserts that social hierarchies existed from the Early Yayoi period and that a multi-layered, pyramid-shaped coalition of chiefs was first established in the northern Kyūshū region and then in the Kinki region during the Middle Yayoi period. Negita (2019: 241) characterizes a hierarchical or stratified society by socially structured inequality, where groups of individuals are unequal, and wealth, prestige, and power are not distributed equally. Matsugi (1995) similarly explains the delay in the emergence of group stratification and dominance-subjugation based on armed conflict. While these phenomena occurred in northern Kyūshū during the Early Yayoi period, they took place in Kinai 畿内, Setouchi 瀬戸内, and Tōkai 東海 during the Late Yayoi period.

In recent decades, the importance of managing the distribution of iron materials and tools has been emphasized in relation to the development of social inequality during the Middle and Late Yayoi periods. Scholars tend to link the rise in social stratification to the transformation of the reciprocal trade networks, associated with the stone tool material sources of the Jōmon period, into a more centralized trade system dependent on obtaining iron materials and tools from external sources (Ando 2008; Matsugi 1996, 2007; Negita 2019; Shitara 2022). From the Jōmon period onwards, trade zones were established within certain areas, starting from the stone material sources for stone tools. However, because iron tools and materials originated from the continent, obtaining them required a broader and new distribution network. Although there is a regional time lag, this transition occurred at some point during the Middle to Late Yayoi period.

Late Yayoi corresponds to a time of significant changes in political power and organization on the Asian continent. This period coincides with the transition from the Western Han 西漢 to the Xin 新 Dynasty and the establishment of the Eastern Han 東漢 Dynasty in China. The Lelang Commandery 楽浪郡, established in 108 BC on the Korean Peninsula, played an important role in Yayoi society. Through this commandery, Yayoi society was able to engage in direct negotiations with the Chinese Han 漢 Dynasty, establishing foreign trade routes (Takaku 2011). The control over technological negotiations and material distribution related to iron production on the Korean Peninsula was closely linked to the administration of the commandery by the Han Dynasty, especially from the Late Han period onwards (Murakami 2007: 292–293). By incorporating the southern half of the Lelang Commandery and its surrounding areas, the Daifang Commandery 帯方郡 was established in the early third century as an administrative division of the Han dynasty. Chinese dynasties introduced their culture and technology through these commanderies to the regimes that existed on the Korean Peninsula and the Japanese archipelago. Late Yayoi society continued direct diplomatic negotiations with the Chinese government, as well as long-distance trade with the continent and the Korean Peninsula.

Shitara (2022) argues that external dependency on iron materials and the relative rise in the status of chiefs advanced social stratification in the Middle Yayoi period. Until then, prominent households had not yet been established, and society was in a state of immature social stratification in the Japanese archipelago. Based on the occurrence of warfare, the presence of weapons as grave goods, and strengthened connections with the Korean Peninsula and China through the Lelang Commandery, Shitara explains that men who participated in wars gained power, leading to the formation of hierarchical structures among regional leaders and their surrounding areas. The chiefs' authority was further enhanced by strengthening connections with people who migrated from the continent. As iron tools became predominant, obtaining iron materials and tools required acquisition from China and the Korean Peninsula. The external dependency on iron materials led to the relative rise in the status of chiefs who controlled distribution, thereby promoting social stratification. According to Shitara's argument, the Middle Yayoi period marks the critical transition from a heterarchical to a hierarchical society. However, Shitara also mentions that in some regions, long-distance exchange, exemplified by the distribution of iron tools, became more prominent after the Late Yayoi period (2017: 539).

Negita (2019)'s study on the ironization of tools in the Kinki region places the timing of this process in the Late Yayoi period. By periodizing the process of ironization in this region, Negita defines the early to middle phase of the Late Yayoi period as the time when primary tools transitioned from stone to iron, and the late phase of the Late Yayoi period as the time when ironization was fully achieved. Negita considers the Late Yayoi period a major turning point that transformed the distribution system and believes that those who controlled the distribution of iron tools formed the upper echelons of society. On the other hand, Murakami 村上 (2007: 297–299) argues that, while iron tool production began in northern Kyūshū along the Sea of Japan coast and toward the Setouchi region in the Middle Yayoi period, other regions, including the Kantō region, had not yet reached a fully ironized stage by the end of the Yayoi period. Murakami asserts that within Yayoi culture, there were no specialized craftsmen dedicated to iron production, and iron did not become a material that generated power relationships on a wide scale.

3 Archaeological Perspectives on Economic Inequality

In the past fifteen years, numerous archaeological studies have made significant advances in the theories and methodologies related to wealth inequality in various parts of the world. For example, Borgerhoff Mulder and colleagues (2009) identify three types of wealth that can be passed down across generations: embodied, relational, and material. Embodied wealth includes attributes, such as body weight, grip strength, knowledge, practical skills, and reproductive success. Relational wealth refers mainly to social connections within networks for sharing food and information. In ancient societies, material wealth was reflected in assets, such as land, livestock, houses, and household goods. These three types of wealth are interrelated and often function in combination. Among them, material wealth has been the most frequently used in archaeological research, typically assessed at the household level through tangible assets, such as house size, domestic storage capacity, and household items. Fargher et al. (2020: 2–3) further define household material wealth as "the sum of intangible assets (e.g., human capital, mineral rights, rights to tribute or corvée, leaseholds, financial assets, cash, etc.) and tangible (physical) assets less liabilities" held by a household.

In agrarian societies, material wealth is typically considered to be more unequally distributed and more strongly transmitted across generations than embodied and relational wealth (Borgerhoff Mulder et al. 2009; Bowles et al. 2010; Smith et al. 2010). By measuring the degree of intergenerational transmission of these three types of wealth, these works have examined the relationship between wealth types and different production systems (hunter-gatherers, horticulturalists, pastoralists, and agriculturalists). Production systems influence the forms of wealth that are transmitted, contributing to the persistence of economic inequality in premodern societies. These works conclude that in ancient agricultural and pastoralist societies, material wealth is the most significant form of wealth, exhibiting the greatest disparity among households and the highest transmissibility between generations.

The traditional social evolutionist notion that the evolution of inequality is closely associated with increased social complexity is still upheld by many. Archaeologists link the emergence of inequalities to increased complexity in various aspects, such as social class and stratification, urbanization, occupational specialization, political structure, and modes of production. Research that suggests a close association between the evolution of persistent wealth inequality and increased social complexity largely focuses on the transition to an agricultural economy and intensified food production. Bar-Yosef (2001) explores the transformation from mobile foragers to settled agricultural communities in Southwest Asia, highlighting the resulting social changes, including private property, territorial control, and social inequality. Kohler and colleagues (2017) observe that increased wealth disparities coincide with the domestication of plants and animals, larger settlement sizes, and growing sociopolitical complexity in their extensive studies across North American, Mesoamerican, and Eurasian sites. Porčić (2019) attributes the rise in social complexity, including the intensification of subsistence production and craft and exchange activities, to social inequalities in the Balkans, covering 6500 to 4200 BC. Similarly, Bogaard et al. (2018, 2019) identify intensified forms of subsistence production, such as land-limited farming, as a major factor in the emergence of persistent inequality from the Neolithic to the Iron Age and Roman period in Western Asia and Europe.

In a related vein to the transition to agricultural settlements and intensified subsistence production, some archaeological research emphasizes the concepts of defendable and transmissible resources as central to the causation of wealth differentials (Abbott et al. 2021; Arponen et al. 2015; Chesson and Goodale 2014; Gurven et al. 2010; Kohler and Higgins 2016; Mattison et al. 2016; Shenk et al. 2010; Smith et al. 2010; Thompson et al. 2021). This notion, influenced by factors such as population increase and resource shortage, underscores the importance of accessing and monopolizing valuable, productive, and defendable resources such as land, labor, surplus, livestock, water supply, exchange networks, and ritual practices. Mattison et al. (2016) highlight the transmissibility of these defendable resources across generations in the evolution of institutionalized inequality. Kohler and Higgins (2016) contend that significant levels of economic inequality arise from resource shortages, especially a lack of arable land in agricultural societies. This scarcity prompts the development and enforcement of private ownership over land, cultivated crops, and stored food. Efficient intergenerational wealth transmission then entrenches these persistent inequalities. In this approach, some researchers emphasize the role of surplus resources as the primary drivers for the creation and maintenance of inequality in antiquity (Hayden and Guy 2024; Morehart and De Lucia 2015; Pailes 2014; Wright 2014). Others highlight that access to ritual space and possession of ritual knowledge played a significant role in establishing and sustaining inequality (Abbott et al. 2021; Borgerhoff Mulder et al. 2009; Vésteinsson et al. 2019).

In recent years, an increasing number of archaeologists adopting an anarchist perspective have challenged the conventional view that social inequality is an inevitable stage in the development of increasingly complex societies (Beck and Quinn 2022; Black Trowel Collective 2016; Borck and Sanger 2017; Fargher et al. 2020; Flexner and Gonzalez-Tennant 2018; González-Ruibal 2025; Graeber and Wengrow 2021; Green 2021; Green et al. 2023; Klinkenberg and Düring 2023; Politopoulos et al. 2024; Semple and Coelho 2022; Wengrow et al. 2025). Graeber and Wengrow (2021) argue that neither agriculture nor urbanization inevitably led to social inequality. They reject the idea of a unilinear evolutionary progression in which human societies transition from foraging to farming, then to urbanization, and ultimately to hierarchical governance. Instead, they emphasize that many societies moved fluidly between these stages or followed alternative trajectories altogether, underscoring that social forms were often the result of deliberate choices rather than predetermined developments. Similarly, Politopoulos and colleagues (2024) demonstrate that anarchist archaeology challenges the assumption that hierarchy is a natural or necessary outcome of social evolution. Instead, it highlights the ways in which people have actively resisted hierarchical structures and illuminates the achievements of egalitarian societies, thereby questioning the naturalness of contemporary power structures and pointing to alternative models for more equitable social relations. González-Ruibal (2025) also notes a growing scholarly interest in egalitarianism and egalitarian practices in complex societies, shaped in part by anarchist perspectives and collective action theory. González-Ruibal argues that Sub-Saharan Africa, with its long history of diverse societies that have either rejected political centralization outright or imposed limits on it, serves as a particularly compelling case within this theoretical framework.

This study supports this perspective and does not regard the development of inequality as an essential and inevitable process toward the formation of complex societies. Rather than assuming the rise of wealth disparities as a natural course in human history, this study aims to empirically assess how wealth inequality expanded, contracted, or remained relatively stable from the Jōmon through the Yayoi periods. Instead of following a unilinear trajectory of increasing inequality, the Jōmon and Yayoi societies reveal both upward and downward fluctuations in wealth disparity. In my future research, I will examine how fluctuations in wealth disparity were shaped by factors such as communal governance, changes in settlement organization, the advent of agricultural practices, and the growth of trade networks centered on iron tools.

4 Measuring Material Wealth in Archaeology

The emergence and development of wealth disparity between households or settlements is archaeologically observable, allowing researchers to trace and compare it across different times and regions. In recent years, scholars have analyzed the development of wealth disparity on a macro scale, employing spatial analyses across extensive geographical regions, temporal analyses to elucidate diachronic changes, or a combination of both (Augereau 2022; Basri and Lawrence 2020; Bogaard et al. 2019; Borgerhoff Mulder et al. 2009; Fochesato et al. 2019; Gurven et al. 2010; Kohler et al. 2017; Munson and Scholnick 2022;

Porčić 2019; Schroder et al. 2023; Shenk et al. 2010; Squitieri and Altaweel 2022; Stone 2018). Basri and Lawrence (2020), for example, extended their research to include a comparative analysis of material wealth inequality between rural and urban settlements in the Ancient Near East. Other researchers have focused on the extent of household wealth disparities at single-site levels (Barnard 2021; Hutson 2016; McLellan and Haines 2023; Nishimura 2023; Oravkinová and Vladár 2020; Pailes 2014; Panitz-Cohen 2011; Prentiss et al. 2018; Simelius 2023).

Methodologically, investigations into the degree of wealth inequality in ancient societies largely rely on quantitative and distributive patterns of accumulated household material culture. Archaeologists have utilized various wealth indicators based on household material culture to measure economic inequality. These indicators include grave architecture and goods, household storage size and capacity, house size, domestic artifacts, and labor costs and material volume for house construction. In the past decade, using house size as an indicator of wealth has become a common practice for analyzing ancient settlements, as the household is the most basic social unit of analysis (e.g., Basri and Lawrence 2020; Bogaard et al. 2024; Kohler and Smith 2018; Kohler et al. 2017; Hutson et al. 2021; Porčić 2019; Schroder et al. 2023; Squitieri and Altaweel 2022). Archaeologists use the sizes of houses and living spaces as reliable proxies to measure the degree of wealth inequality at various settlements worldwide. This proxy is favored due to its geographical and temporal comparability, based on the assumption that larger households generally have more resources and wealth.

The validity of house size as a meaningful proxy in ancient communities has been widely discussed. Kohler et al. (2017) argue for the usefulness of house size as a wealth indicator based on extensive data gathered from various ancient societies globally. They support their claim using ethnographic documentation and by cross-examining household wealth estimates obtained through different proxies in previous studies. Strawinska-Zanko et al. (2018: 165–169) also examine house size as a proxy in their analysis of wealth distribution across four Maya archaeological sites. They justify this method by the consistent correlation between wealth levels and house sizes in agrarian states, despite potential confounding factors such as location, zoning, and family size. Stone (2018: 233) points out a caveat that, unless houses are relatively free-standing structures, isolating individual dwelling units with shared party walls in crowded residential areas is challenging without fine-grained excavations.

There are also archaeological studies that measure household wealth disparity based on domestic artifacts (e.g., Borgerhoff Mulder et al. 2009; Hutson 2016; Kim 2025; Nishimura 2023, 2025; Olson and Smith 2016; Oravkinová and Vladár 2020; Panitz-Cohen 2011; Porčić 2019; Prentiss et al. 2018; Smith 1987; Smith et al. 2010; Wright 2014). In many of these studies, the degree of inequality is assessed through a combination of household inventories and house sizes. The types of domestic artifacts included in these studies are primarily pots, copper items, figurines, amulets, loom weights, flints, mace-heads, and grinding stones.

This study assumes that in the settled communities of the Jōmon and Yayoi periods, the floor area of a house is proportional to the level of wealth held by the household. Based on contemporary data from the areas where the majority of archaeological sites examined in this study are concentrated (namely, Kōhoku 港北, Tsuzuki 都筑, Aoba 青葉, and Midori 緑 Wards in Yokohama 横浜 City), I investigated whether a proportional relationship exists between household income and living space (Table 1). This dataset has been compiled and edited by the City of Yokohama, based solely on the summary tables published by the Statistics Bureau of the Ministry of Internal Affairs and Communications that include data on Yokohama's administrative wards (City of Yokohama, Policy Bureau 2020). Drawing on the data from a total of 423,950 modern primary households across these wards, I used simple linear regression to analyze the relationship between annual household income, defined as the combined yearly income of all household members, and living space, measured as total tatami 畳 mat area, with one tatami mat equivalent to 1.65 m². The analysis revealed a strong positive correlation between household income level and the average size of living space per household across all income brackets, regardless of whether the dwelling was owned or rented. Specifically, strong positive correlations were observed in each of the four wards: Kōhoku Ward ($r^2 = 0.85$, two-sided $p = 0.0004$), Midori Ward ($r^2 = 0.91$, two-sided $p = 0.0001$), Aoba Ward ($r^2 = 0.95$, two-sided $p = 0.0001$), and Tsuzuki Ward ($r^2 = 0.91$, two-sided $p = 0.0001$). These findings indicate a clear proportional relationship between household income and residential space in the region. On this basis, the present study posits that variations in dwelling size during the Jōmon and Yayoi periods may similarly reflect disparities in household wealth.

The representative dwelling type in these periods is the pit dwelling, which involved digging an elliptical or circular hole in the ground, erecting pillars at the bottom of the hole, and supporting a roof with these pillars. Assuming that the typical Jōmon pit dwelling had an area of twenty square meters, Shitara (2014: 54–58) believes that groups of a nuclear family size resided in them. The residents of pit dwellings were centered around a married couple, but the existence of larger pit dwellings with multiple hearths also suggests the possibility of extended families or the cohabitation of multiple households. Regarding post-marriage residence rules and descent regulations, Shitara finds a patrilineal tendency in the Kantō region from the Late Jōmon period onward. Regarding family composition during the Yayoi period, Wei Zhi's account of

Table 1 Income levels, number of households, and average living space size (measured in tatami mats) in the four wards of Yokohama City (City of Yokohama, Policy Bureau, General Affairs Division, 2020)

Household income level	Kōhoku ward		Midori ward		Aoba ward		Tsuzuki ward	
	Number of households	Number of Tatami mats	Number of households	Number of Tatami mats	Number of households	Number of Tatami mats	Number of households	Number of Tatami mats
Less than 1 million yen	6,160	18.62	2,250	23.32	5,560	18.57	1,170	21.57
1 to less than 2 million yen	10,870	21.68	6,850	22.36	7,380	26.45	4,410	23.33
2 to less than 3 million yen	20,660	22.57	11,120	24.92	14,290	28.27	7,620	26.88
3 to less than 4 million yen	21,780	24.77	10,460	26.84	15,610	28.4	8,040	29.44
4 to less than 5 million yen	18,220	23.36	9,130	28.34	13,740	31.52	7,390	29.17
5 to less than 7 million yen	29,440	27.89	12,960	30.49	19,790	33.84	14,060	31.44
7 to less than 10 million yen	27,890	32.57	12,640	33.92	22,340	36.56	15,850	35.34
10 to less than 15 million yen	14,770	38.17	6,080	38.5	15,040	41.03	11,580	39.84
15 million yen or more	4,900	47.75	1,550	44.7	8,130	46.45	4,220	48.01

the Wa people states that the "Father, mother, and older and younger siblings sleep separately" (Saeki 2018: 123). The pit dwellings from the Jōmon and Yayoi periods were built as freestanding structures without shared walls, making it relatively easy to calculate the floor area of each individual unit. At many archaeological sites, dozens of such dwellings have been excavated, their floor areas measured, and the resulting data published. As long as the stratigraphy has not been significantly disturbed, the original dimensions of a dwelling's floor area can often be recovered with a high degree of confidence. Moreover, floor area is the only type of archaeological data in this region that allows for meaningful comparisons across different sites and time periods.

Factors such as village size, landscape conditions, and the availability of building materials likely influenced house size. Therefore, it is not possible to combine data across different sites, and the degree of wealth disparity must be calculated separately for each site. While house size is also assumed to be influenced by other factors, such as the number of people living in the household, this study measures wealth at the household level rather than the individual level. Whether a large house is occupied by a large family or a small one, it is assumed that the total wealth represented by that larger house exceeds that of households occupying smaller homes within the same settlement. Therefore, it is the total wealth mobilized to construct and maintain the dwelling, rather than the number of inhabitants, that is considered the key variable.

However, there have been numerous criticisms of the conventional definition of wealth as merely accumulated assets. For example, Kay et al. (2023) question the traditional approach that links material accumulation to social power and status, arguing that it implicitly projects modern capitalist theory onto prehistoric societies. They call for more context-specific practices and an understanding of the social meanings behind material accumulations. Rakopoulos and Rio (2018) also challenge the conventional financial definition of wealth, arguing that wealth is embedded in social and cultural contexts and should be understood in its relational and reproductive aspects, such as social connections, knowledge, and cultural heritage. Similarly, Arponen et al. (2015) criticize traditional market-based measures of inequality, considering the focus on the distribution of material goods insufficient. They suggest a capability approach, which considers what individuals are able to do and be, rather than merely what they possess. These researchers seek a more nuanced and multifaceted understanding of wealth inequality in specific cultural and historical contexts, incorporating factors such as individual actions and practices, social networks and relationships, and environmental and ecological contexts into their theoretical frameworks.

Regardless of which economic indicators researchers use, many frequently incorporate simple statistical models to quantitatively measure the degree of wealth inequality for spatial and temporal comparisons. Smith et al. (2014: 312) state that Randall McGuire first introduced the Gini index to archaeology in 1983, noting a minor surge in its applications among archaeologists by 2014. Since then, the Gini coefficient has become a key instrument for quantifying wealth inequality in archaeological research (e.g., Bogaard et al. 2024; Chase 2017; Klinkenberg and Düring 2023; Kohler and Smith 2018; McCoy and Panuska 2024; Siteleki and Fredriksen 2024; Smith et al. 2014; Windler et al. 2013; Yu et al. 2019). The Gini coefficient ranges from 0, representing perfect equality, to 1, representing perfect inequality. Gini coefficients are calculated by plotting the cumulative share of wealth or income against the cumulative share of the population, creating a curve that is compared to a line of perfect equality. The more the curve deviates from this line, the greater the inequality. It indicates the material wealth disparity among specific units of study, such as houses in a neighborhood, neighborhoods in a settlement, and settlements in a region. When sample sizes are small, these studies tend to use Gini coefficients with bootstrapping to attach error ranges to Gini values at certain confidence levels. While the Gini coefficient quantifies the extent of wealth inequality, it does not reveal specifics about how economic inequality manifests or evolves within a society.

The Lorenz curves, which form the basis for the Gini values, visualize the wealth share against certain percentiles of the population. On a Lorenz curve graph, a straight line represents a perfectly equal distribution of wealth across a population, while a curved line depicts the actual distribution of wealth within the population. When the curved line deviates farther from the straight line, it depicts a more unequal distribution. The shape of the curved line indicates what percentile of the population holds what percentile of the total wealth present within the population. The use of the Lorenz curve supplements the Gini coefficient, illuminating the distribution of wealth among households. Especially when combined with relevant literature, it can shed light on the form of wealth disparity within each site or occupation level.

Since the Gini coefficient was determined to be the most appropriate statistical method for this study, I used the Gini module in StatsDirect to calculate unbiased estimators of the population Gini, using house size as a proxy for economic status. I then compared levels of material wealth disparity across different time periods and sites. To improve the robustness of the results, I applied a bootstrapping method with 100,000 replicates and reported error ranges for each Gini coefficient. This approach enhances confidence at the 95 percent level by capturing a broader range of possible Gini values.

5 Issues with Quantification of Material Wealth

There are several issues associated with applying quantitative economic comparisons in archaeology. One significant challenge is expressing ancient household wealth in numerical terms. Archaeologists need a standardized and objective method for measuring household wealth that can be applied and compared across different houses, sites, regions, and time periods. While converting various types of material wealth, such as house sizes and storage capacities, into numerical forms (e.g., square meters or cubic meters) is relatively straightforward, other aspects can be more complex. Some researchers extend their efforts to compute the architectural volume or the labor cost of constructing dwellings to assess the amount of labor invested in household construction (Abbott et al. 2021; Chase 2017).

The computation becomes more complicated for the economic values across other types of material culture, such as ceramic pots, stone tools, jewelry items, metal objects, ovens, benches, and stone-paved floors. Is one small bead made of glass equivalent to a bead made of gold? Should each small stone bead be counted as one artifact, even though a group of these beads may have belonged to a chain necklace? A small, undecorated clay cup probably did not have an equivalent economic value to an intricately painted large storage jar. All these values are contingent on the historical context of the society in which these objects were found—how difficult it was to obtain or make the object, and how much it was actually valued in the society.

Using domestic artifacts from three Aztec-period settlements, Olson and Smith (2016) developed two wealth indices: one that is context-specific and another that is a more generic measure to evaluate the value of household artifacts. Both indices effectively distinguished between elite and commoner households using domestic artifacts, such as ceramic serving wares and stone tools. Using grave goods, Stone (2018) and Munson and Scholnick (2022) exemplify the quantification of the economic values of a wide range of objects found in mortuary contexts. With aid from the textual record, Stone (2018: 255) weighed and converted burial items made of gold, copper, and bronze into the ancient Mesopotamian currency. The values of other, more common objects made of stone and clay were estimated in the same currency based on the cost of the material and labor to make these artifacts. Applying and modifying Stone's work, Nishimura (2025) compared values of household inventories by assigning a relative value in copper weight to each artifact type at houses excavated at Tell Asmar and Khafajah, in central Mesopotamia. Munson and Scholnick (2022) divided burial goods in Ancient Maya into three categories—personal ornaments for individual wealth, utilitarian objects for supra-household wealth, and ritual items. Their method is a simple count of these grave goods, totaling the number of various types of objects in each category. However, in archaeological studies of burials, scholars argue that sheer quantity may be misleading, as large numbers of common items often hold less value than a few rare ones; therefore, alternative methods are used to adjust for qualitative differences and to prevent ubiquitous objects from disproportionately inflating overall grave values (Flad 2002; Jörgensen 1988).

Another issue with applying quantitative economic comparisons is the bias in data introduced through formation processes. Domestic floor assemblages are subject to depositional biases, particularly because household objects and waste are movable (LaMotta and Schiffer 1999; Simelius 2023; Smith 1987). Built-in architectural features and household items would have experienced varied formation processes during the course of house occupation. Therefore, there is no guarantee that the archaeological remains reflect the total wealth of the household at a specific time period. Unless a detailed analysis of formation processes in a particular context is feasible, research must be based on the premise that material remains preserved and excavated from floor levels within houses are not completely random but reflect the material culture used and abandoned by the occupants. To mitigate concerns about formation processes, household inventories and architectural features need to come from primary floor contexts. It is also essential to cross-examine wealth through multiple economic variables, such as house size, domestic features, and household artifacts. Using different variables helps cross-check biases in data and may also reflect household wealth at different times during the house's use.

There has been debate about the cross-cultural reliability of various wealth indices. For example, researchers have noticed discrepancies in the degree of material wealth inequality when comparing house size and grave goods as proxies. Porčić (2019) reports that grave goods show much higher inequality values than household items at multiple archaeological sites in the Balkans. Similarly, Fochesato et al. (2019: 860) and Stone (2018: 255–256) describe that grave goods consistently indicate higher economic disparity than house sizes. This discrepancy possibly arises from the tendency of burial data to represent individuals, whereas house data reflect households (Fochesato et al. 2019: 860; Porčić 2019: 374; Smith et al. 2014: 313). Stone (2018: 256) also points out that wealth disparity is heightened with grave goods because, while house sizes fall within a certain range to function as living spaces, funerary data do not have such limits when quantified. Kay et al. (2023) argue that burials created social value and differentiated individuals in social relationships, suggesting that burials did not necessarily correlate with the accumulation of power or wealth.

Although the issue of incomparability between funerary and house data in quantitative economic comparisons is significant, the use of burial data as a proxy for inequality remains prevalent in archaeological literature over the last decade (e.g., Augereau 2022; Bogaard et al. 2019; Coupland et al. 2016; Gibbons 2019; Mittnik et al. 2019; Munson and Scholnick 2022; Osterholtz and Valent 2025; Vila et al. 2015; Windler et al. 2013; Yu et al. 2019). Fochesato et al. (2019: 860), for instance, argue that inequality measures based on grave goods are highly correlated with those based on house size. They developed a conversion method to adjust the higher Gini values in burial data to those in household data and concluded that it is fruitful to combine burial data with other proxies as a multidimensional approach to measure the differential distribution of material wealth at the household level.

The problem of incomparability between different wealth indices is also evident in quantitative analyses, particularly when comparing house size with storage capacity, or when household size is measured using different metrics, such as floor area (m^2) versus volume (m^3). Some studies that employed household storage size and capacity as wealth indicators explain that storage capacity is more unequally distributed since it reflects anticipated household income, such as harvested crops of the year, rather than total household wealth (Bogaard et al. 2018; Kohler and Higgins 2016). Ames and Grier (2020: 1043) also observe discrepancies in the degree of material wealth inequality between house size and storage capacity, noting that residential storage size and capacity consistently show higher degrees of unequal wealth distribution than house size. They conclude that household storage capacity is not a reliable indicator of wealth differences or anticipated income, as it reflects the residents' strategies for using their food surplus. Similarly, research by Thompson and colleagues (2023) demonstrates that both the choice of measurement unit (area vs. volume) and the unit of analysis (e.g., individual structures, all structures within a household group, or the entire group including surrounding space) have a significant impact on the resulting Gini coefficient and, consequently, on how inequality is interpreted.

Lastly, another issue occasionally noted in the application of quantitative economic comparisons is that conventional methods do not analyze what wealth disparity means in ancient societies. The recent wave of archaeological investigations into material wealth inequality has encountered a countercurrent that calls for considering the human experience and quality of life of ancient people (Dennehy et al. 2016; Fochesato et al. 2019; Hutson 2016; Hutson et al. 2021; Kuijt 2024; Munson and Scholnick 2022; Vésteinsson et al. 2019; Wilkinson 2019). Quantitative comparisons of accumulated material wealth, including statistical tools such as the Gini coefficient, illuminate the degree of material wealth disparity between individuals, households, and neighborhoods in ancient societies. However, these comparisons do not analyze how material wealth was distributed or how the owners and users of the material wealth experienced wealth inequality. Fochesato et al. (2019: 855) explain this point by highlighting that "two identical Gini coefficients measuring wealth inequality may even be associated with radically different distributions of wealth—for example, one in which inequality arises from a small concentration of entirely property-less households at the bottom of an otherwise relatively equal (in terms of wealth) population and the other with a few exceptionally rich households in a population of small landowners." Using the capability approach, this perspective gravitates toward the social well-being of ancient people through other types of wealth inequality, incorporating factors such as access to rituals, critical items, and public services. Dennehy et al. (2016) focus on the spatial distribution and accessibility of urban services (such as markets, religious facilities, and assembly spaces) in six premodern cities. They find that elite neighborhoods had better access to urban services, indicating systemic inequality in urban service provision. Lower-status residents typically had less access to these services, negatively impacting their daily lives and overall quality of life. Residents in peripheral neighborhoods often faced greater travel distances to access essential services, reducing their time for other productive activities.

While ideally wealth inequality would be assessed using multiple economic proxies, this case study, like many others in archaeological research, faces a lack of alternative data sources in the region. Items such as high-value goods reliably associated with individual households, burials linked to specific dwellings, or spatial data based on dwelling volume beyond just floor area are largely unavailable. This is a common challenge in archaeological contexts, where preservation conditions and taphonomic processes often limit the types of data that can be meaningfully recovered. Nevertheless, using the floor area of pit dwellings as the primary material wealth indicator has a major advantage: the sheer volume of published data. This includes a large number of pit dwellings and a wide range of archaeological sites, allowing for meaningful analysis of broader patterns across the Late Jōmon, Middle Yayoi, and Late Yayoi periods, as well as across the individual sites in the study region. Compared to other types of archaeological data, such as portable artifacts, floor area is also considered less vulnerable to site formation processes in this region. This is particularly true given the widely reported scarcity of features and artifacts recovered from the floors of pit dwellings dating to these time periods.

Although the Gini coefficient can measure levels of wealth inequality at each settlement during the Jōmon and Yayoi periods, it does not directly tell us what that inequality meant for the people who lived there, such as their lived experiences, challenges, or opportunities. However, what it can offer is a view of inequality patterns over the long term and across the entire study region. This case study aims to go further by pairing Gini coefficients with Lorenz curves and scatter plots to visualize these patterns more clearly. Through this approach, it becomes possible to gain insight into what the measured degrees of inequality may have meant for the communities that inhabited these dwellings.

6 The Study Area in the Southern Kantō Region

To examine the evolution of material wealth disparity, measured by house floor size in residential neighborhoods, I gathered data from settlements dating from the Late Jōmon to Late Yayoi period (ca. 2540 BC–AD 250) within the southern Kantō region (Figure 2 and Table 2). These sites are located in the border region between the northeast of modern-day Kanagawa 神奈川 Prefecture and the

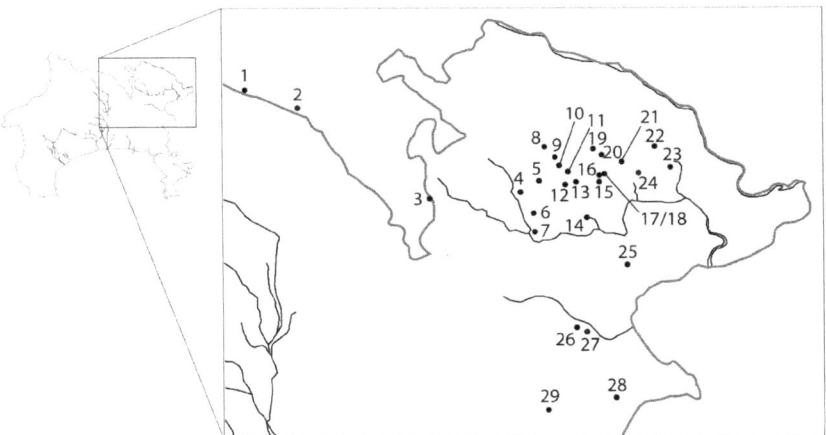

Figure 2 Map showing the archaeological sites analyzed in this study, located along the border of northeastern Kanagawa Prefecture and southern Tōkyō.
1 = Tama New Town #245; 2 = Tama New Town #194; 3 = Nasunahara;
4 = Sannomaru; 5 = Keshōdai; 6 = Kawawa-Mukaihara; 7 = Haradeguchi;
8 = Kanpukuji/Kanpukuji-Kita; 9 = E5; 10 = Hachimanyama;
11 = Ōtsuka; 12 = Komaru; 13 = Tsunasakiyama; 14 = Orimoto-Nishihara;
15 = Oppara; 16 = Gondappara; 17 = Kitagawa; 18 = Kitagawa-Omotenoue;
19 = Yamada-Ōtsuka; 20 = Okkoshi; 21 = Terayato; 22 = Kaniwa/Idaisedai;
23 = Hiyoshidai; 24 = Moritohara; 25 = Shinohara-Ōharakita; 26 = Bukkō;
27 = Myōjindai; 28 = Santonodai; 29 = Tonoyashiki.

Table 2 The list of Jōmon and Yayoi archaeological sites included in the present study

Site Name	Site Name in Japanese	Location
Bukkō	仏向	Yokohama City, Kanagawa
E5	E5	Yokohama City, Kanagawa
Gondappara	権田原	Yokohama City, Kanagawa
Hachimanyama	八幡山	Yokohama City, Kanagawa
Haradeguchi	原出口	Yokohama City, Kanagawa
Hiyoshidai	日吉台	Yokohama City, Kanagawa
Kaniwa/Idaisedai	神庭・井田伊勢台	Kawasaki City, Kanagawa
Kanpukuji/Kanpukuji-Kita	観福寺北	Yokohama City, Kanagawa
Kawawa-Mukaihara	川和向原	Yokohama City, Kanagawa
Keshōdai	華蔵台	Yokohama City, Kanagawa
Kitagawa	北川貝塚	Yokohama City, Kanagawa
Kitagawa-Omotenoue	北川表の上	Yokohama City, Kanagawa
Komaru	小丸	Yokohama City, Kanagawa
Moritohara	森戸原	Yokohama City, Kanagawa
Myōjindai	明神台	Yokohama City, Kanagawa
Nasunahara	なすな原	Machida City, Tokyo
Okkoshi	打越	Yokohama City, Kanagawa
Oppara	大原	Yokohama City, Kanagawa
Orimoto-Nishihara	折本西原	Yokohama City, Kanagawa

Table 2 (cont.)

Site Name	Site Name in Japanese	Location
Ōtsuka	大塚	Yokohama City, Kanagawa
Sannomaru	三の丸	Yokohama City, Kanagawa
Santonodai	三殿台	Yokohama City, Kanagawa
Shinohara-Ōharakita	篠原大原北	Yokohama City, Kanagawa
Tama New Town #194	多摩ニュータウン#194	Machida City, Tokyo
Tama New Town #245	多摩ニュータウン#245	Machida City, Tokyo
Terayato	寺谷戸	Yokohama City, Kanagawa
Tonoyashiki	殿屋敷	Yokohama City, Kanagawa
Tsunasakiyama	綱崎山	Yokohama City, Kanagawa
Yamada-Ōtsuka	山田大塚	Yokohama City, Kanagawa
Kiusu 5	キウス5遺跡	Chitose City, Hokkaidō
Kiusu 5 and 7	キウス5・7遺跡	Chitose City, Hokkaidō

southern part of Tōkyō 東京 Metropolis. This area is ideal for investigation due to extensive excavations, such as those in Kōhoku New Town and Tama 多摩 New Town, which revealed a large number of completely excavated pit houses at many nearby settlements. More than half of the sites come from Kōhoku New Town, while the rest are from adjacent areas.

It is widely acknowledged that the cultural florescence of Middle Jōmon society, particularly in central Honshū 本州, collapsed from the Late Jōmon period (ca. 2540–1270 BC), leading to the dispersion into small settlements (Noxon 2025). The decline in the size and number of settlements is particularly evident after the Final Jōmon period (ca. 1270–250 BC), when settlements became much fewer, smaller, and more decentralized, accompanied by a drastic decrease in the number of pit dwellings (Shitara 2004). This general decrease in the number of dwellings and the scarcity of settlements from Late Jōmon up to Middle Yayoi (ca. 250 BC) have been frequently reported in the study area (e.g., Kanagawa Archaeological Society 2011: 7; Tanabe 2023; Yokohama City Historical Foundation Buried Cultural Property Center 2008: 471, 2009: 2). The cooling climate has been posited as a major factor for these changes, affecting a wide area of the Japanese archipelago, leading to population decline and the downsizing and dispersion of settlements (e.g., Kunikita 2023; Shitara 2004). Another theory attempts to explain the historical evolution after the Late Jōmon period as part of the Eurasian processes of Bronze Age globalization (Hudson et al. 2021). The Bronze Age required new supplies of metal ores and other raw materials, transforming Eurasian trade economies and resulting in trade networks and population dispersals that created new economic forms.

In the southern Kantō region, large-scale wet-rice farming settlements, accompanied by changes in mortuary practices and pottery, began to appear in lowland areas during the middle of the Middle Yayoi period (Nagatomo et al. 2022). The Nakazato 中里 site, located in the Ashigara 足柄 Plain, is one such example. Although large settlements indicating the full-scale onset of agriculture in this region have only been excavated from the latter half of the Middle Yayoi period onward, Ishikawa 石川 (2022: 66–68) argues that the transition to a fully developed rice-farming society had already taken place by the middle of the Middle Yayoi period. This shift encompassed areas from the coast of Sagami 相模 Bay to the eastern shore of Tōkyō Bay and extended into northern Saitama 埼玉 Prefecture. Scholars have debated the extent to which the spread of Yayoi culture and the introduction of fully developed wet-rice agriculture to the Kantō region were influenced by exchange and interaction with surrounding regions, including the Tōkai area, the Chūō 中央 Highlands (including Nagano 長野 Prefecture), and the Kinai region (Nagatomo et al. 2022; Barnes 2019).

According to Ishikawa (2001), by the late Middle Yayoi period, the large wet-rice farming settlements established in the preceding phase had become centers for organizing regional societies and played a key role in the formation of other settlements. During the late phase of Middle Yayoi, fully developed agricultural settlements, including large-scale moated villages with many groups of rectangular encircling moat burials, suddenly appeared in the southern Kantō region, and the concentration of populations became prominent. This state did not last long, as the construction of moat-enclosed settlements collapsed around the first half of the Late Yayoi period, leading to a sudden decrease in settlements. Nevertheless, in the latter half of the Late Yayoi period, settlements rapidly increased again in this region, with super-large settlements emerging due to significant population concentration (Kobayashi et al. 2022: 12).

Yayoi Period Research Project Team (2011) provides an overview of the emergence and development of ironware in Kanagawa Prefecture, including the region examined in this study. They state that ironware first appeared in Kanagawa during the latter half of the Middle Yayoi period. The iron artifacts unearthed from this stage mainly consist of flat iron axes, along with agricultural tools, such as chisels and small knives. From the Late Yayoi period onward, iron swords and iron bracelets began to appear and were found as grave goods in large burial mounds. This suggests that ironware came to be used not only to enhance productive capacity, but also as weapons and ornaments. In the study region, bronze artifacts, such as rings and bracelets, appear in the Late Yayoi period, but their numbers are extremely limited.

In the early Kofun period, after approximately AD 250, the settlements in this region generally declined, with few exceptions, such as the Terayato 寺谷戸 site (Yokohama City Historical Foundation Buried Cultural Property Center 2009: 356). No significant early Kofun tombs have been found in this area, suggesting that the political centers of the Kofun period did not emerge from the Yayoi settlements.

7 Data

In this investigation, I used house floor area (in square meters) as an indicator of wealth. Due to the lack of sufficient artifacts or structural remains on pit dwelling floors for meaningful comparison, house size served as the only viable proxy for wealth disparity. For comparative purposes, I selected Jōmon and Yayoi period settlements with a sufficient number of excavated residential structures whose floor areas (in square meters) or dimensions (main and secondary axes in meters) are published in excavation reports. Specifically, data were gathered from 265 houses at 10 Late Jōmon (ca. 2540–1270 BC) settlements, 11 houses at 1 Final Jōmon (ca. 1270–250 BC) settlement, 368 houses at 7 late-Middle Yayoi (ca. 100 BC–AD 1) settlements, and 506 houses at 16 Late Yayoi (ca. AD 1–250) settlements (Appendix A). Although roughly contemporaneous, these residential structures were not necessarily occupied simultaneously, even at the same site. Although the Final Jōmon period has a limited number of samples and does not allow for reliable comparisons, I categorized the periods into these four stages to examine the levels of wealth disparity. The number of samples with known house sizes at the 10 Late Jōmon sites ranged from 10 to 50, averaging 26.5 houses per site. For the Final Jōmon period, only one site had a sufficient number of houses whose floor areas were known. The number of samples at the 7 Middle Yayoi sites ranged from 14 to 96, averaging 52.6 houses per site. The number of samples at the 16 Late Yayoi sites ranged from 12 to 69, averaging 31.6 houses per site.

Pit dwellings known as "handle-mirror" type structures are occasionally found within archaeological sites, though at a low frequency. They are so named because the entrance area extends outward in a narrow projection, resembling the handle of a hand mirror, giving the overall floor plan the appearance of a mirror with a handle. In the case of pit-dwelling remains of the handle-mirror type, the residential floor area corresponding to the "handle" was excluded from area calculations. This is because such projections are often excluded from area estimates in published reports, and because this type of pit dwelling is rarely found in the data.

House areas reported in excavation records were measured either at the top or bottom of the excavated pit that served as an indoor space. When a ditch surrounding the dwelling was identified, the major and minor axes were often calculated based on the inner or outer edge of the ditch (see (A) in Figure 3). If no surrounding ditch was found, the floor area was sometimes estimated based on the outer edge of a line connecting the postholes (see (B) in Figure 3). Since the criteria for calculating the floor area of a pit dwelling can vary depending on

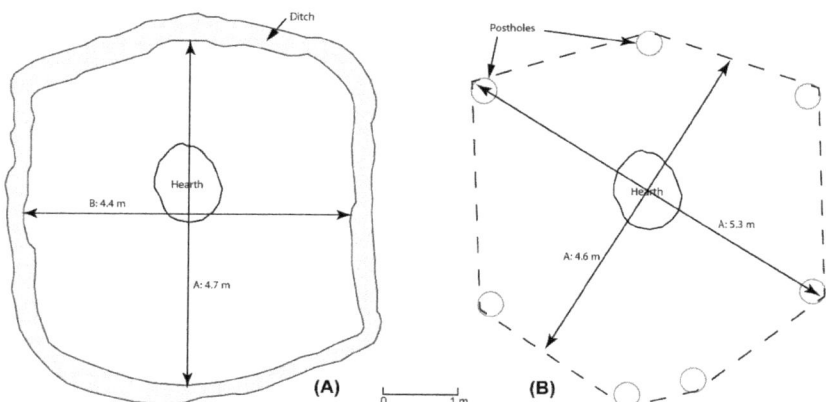

Figure 3 Diagram illustrating the method used to measure the size of pit dwellings. (A): The major axis (the longest dimension) and the minor axis (perpendicular to the major axis) are measured based on the inner edge of the surrounding ditch. (B): Based on the outer edge of the postholes, the longest line is taken as the major axis, and the line perpendicular to it is measured as the minor axis. Most of the reports in this study adopt method (A), while method (B) is rarely used in settlements where surrounding ditches are largely absent.

the excavator or the report's author, it is not possible to combine data derived using different methods to calculate a single Gini coefficient.

For most sites, only the lengths of the major and minor axes were provided, and floor areas were calculated in square meters by multiplying these dimensions. In some cases, excavators estimated the axis lengths from exposed sections of structures that had not been fully excavated. Calculations of wealth disparity based on house size were conducted separately for each site. Only sites with more than ten excavated and consistently measured houses were included in the analysis. Multiple excavation reports from the same residential area were entered separately into the database to avoid skewing the data, particularly when measurement methods differed across reports. When calculating the Gini coefficient for each site, statistically significant differences between reports were considered, resulting in multiple Gini values for the same site when necessary.

In cases where the dating of the houses was not distinctly marked in excavation reports, entries labeled 'Late Yayoi to Incipient Kofun' were counted as Late Yayoi, while those labeled only as 'Incipient Kofun' were excluded. Houses not distinguished between Middle and Late Yayoi, or marked 'Late Yayoi to Early Kofun,' were also excluded unless the vast majority of houses excavated within the same neighborhood were dated to 'Late Yayoi.'

The average area of 265 Late Jōmon houses is 36.3 m². Although there are only 11 houses from the Final Jōmon period, their average area is 33.9 m². This is comparable to the average size of 34.3 m² for 368 Middle Yayoi houses. Therefore, the average house size in this region remains roughly the same or slightly decreases from Late Jōmon to Middle Yayoi. Conversely, the average area of 506 Late Yayoi houses significantly decreases to 26.6 m². During the Late Yayoi period, houses around or smaller than 10 m² became more common. It is unlikely that several family members could live in such small houses. Similarly, while Middle Yayoi pit dwellings predominantly had a long axis of six to eight meters, most of Late Yayoi pit dwellings had a long axis of less than five meters (Kanpukuji-Kita Site Excavation Team 1997: 311–315; Yokohama City Buried Cultural Property Center 1991: 32; Yokohama City Historical Foundation Buried Cultural Property Center 2011: 131).

In the study region, one or two Late Jōmon houses of around 100 m² can be found in a settlement. These include House 18 (94.9 m²) at Komaru 小丸, House 16A (108.6 m²) and House 41 (119.3 m²) at Keshōdai 華蔵台, and House BJ92 (106.7 m²) at Sannomaru 三の丸. In the Late Jōmon period, 'core pit houses,' which might have been inhabited by residents with special status or positions within the settlement, emerged as central structures in villages. Though small in number, these houses were larger and repeatedly rebuilt in the same prominent locations. They were typically situated near cemeteries, suggesting they housed village chiefs or shamans (Ishii 1994). Showing overlapping traces of remodeling in concentric circles, these large houses were generally enlarged through each renovation, with newer versions always being larger in scale.

From the Middle Yayoi period onward, such large houses became increasingly larger. For instance, House Y13A (125.5 m²) at Orimono-Nishihara 折本西原 and House 306 C (133.7 m²) at Santonodai 三殿台 stand out. In the Late Yayoi period, these large houses became even larger, exemplified by House Y32 (244 m²) at Moritohara 森戸原 and House 6 (159.6 m²) at Kanpukuji-Kita 観福寺北. While many large-scale residences grew through continuous expansion, indicating accumulating wealth, some show no traces of reconstruction or rebuilding. This suggests that certain houses, such as House CY2 at Gondappara 権田原 and House 6 at Kanpukuji-Kita/Sekikōchi 関耕地, were constructed as large-scale residences from the beginning.

Large and small houses are distinguished at some sites but not at others. In certain areas of some settlements, a few large houses with a long axis of over nine meters can be found, while at other sites, no particular regularity is observed in the placement of large-scale residences (Kanpukuji-Kita Site Excavation Team 1997: 311–315; Yokohama City Buried Cultural Property Center 1991: 425–426; Yokohama City Buried Cultural Property Investigation Committee 1980: 362–364; Yokohama City Historical Foundation Buried Cultural Property Center 2009: 349–355, 2011: 131–134, 2017: 13). The increasing size and prominence of these large houses over time indicate a disparity in material wealth, but, at most sites, no differences are observed in the internal facilities regardless of the size of the pit dwellings (Takahashi 2024: 30).

8 Results

The average Gini value for the house area calculated for each Late Jōmon site is 0.25 (Table 3). Some sites show higher or lower Gini values within a range of 0.17 to 0.36, but half of the sites have Gini values of 0.23 or 0.24. At the Keshōdai and Nasunahara なすな原 sites, Gini values were derived separately due to potential differences in excavation methods and report formats. However, even when the data were combined, the average Gini value across all ten sites remained unchanged. Relatively small sample sizes, such as ten houses at Tama New Town #194 and nine houses at Nasunahara, do not appear to deviate from the average Gini value. At the Keshōdai site, two Gini coefficients were calculated separately due to differences in excavation areas within the same site, resulting in significantly different values. The Shinohara-Ōharakita 篠原大原北 site's Gini value of 0.17 is noticeably lower than that

Table 3 Gini coefficients for the house area at the Late Jōmon sites

	Number of pit-house	Standard error (bootstrap)	Unbiased estimator of population Gini coefficient	Bias-corrected and accelerated bootstrap 95 percent confidence interval	
				Low	High
1. Yamada-Ōtsuka	28	0.03	0.23	0.20	0.32
2. Keshōdai	36	0.02	0.36	0.33	0.41
	14	0.03	0.20	0.17	0.26
3. Kawawa-Mukaihara	22	0.03	0.24	0.22	0.31
4. Haradeguchi	17	0.03	0.23	0.18	0.29
5. Komaru	32	0.03	0.33	0.29	0.40
6. Sannomaru	21	0.04	0.32	0.27	0.41
7. Shinohara-Ōharakita	29	0.03	0.17	0.14	0.25
8. Tama New Town #245	16	0.03	0.24	0.21	0.35
9. Tama New Town #194	10	0.04	0.24	0.19	0.33
10. Nasunahara	31	0.03	0.21	0.17	0.29
	9	0.04	0.26	0.23	0.33

of other sites, while a few locations, such as Komaru (0.33) and Sannomaru (0.32), show higher values.

The Gini value for the Final Jōmon houses at the Nasunahara site is 0.23 (Table 4). Although this result is provisional, as it concerns only 11 houses at a single site, the Gini value is comparable to, or somewhat lower than, the average value from the Late Jōmon period. The Late Jōmon houses excavated at this site show Gini coefficients of 0.21 and 0.26, indicating no significant difference in the Gini values between these two periods at this site.

The average Gini value for the house area at the Middle Yayoi sites is 0.22 (Table 5). Although similar to the 0.25 of the Late Jōmon period, the average value is slightly lower. Among the seven sites, six have Gini coefficients between 0.19 and 0.23, while the low value at Hachimanyama 八幡山 (0.14) and the relatively high figure at Santonodai (0.31) are notable. The relatively small sample sizes of 14 houses at Hachimanyama and 16 houses at Santonodai

Table 4 Gini coefficient for the house area at the Final Jōmon site

	Number of pit-house	Standard error (bootstrap)	Unbiased estimator of population Gini coefficient	Bias-corrected and accelerated bootstrap 95 percent confidence interval	
				Low	High
1. Nasunahara	11	0.04	0.23	0.19	0.34

Table 5 Gini coefficients for the house area at the Middle Yayoi sites

	Number of pit-house	Standard error (bootstrap)	Unbiased estimator of population Gini coefficient	Bias-corrected and accelerated bootstrap 95 percent confidence interval	
				Low	High
1. Ōtsuka	96	0.02	0.22	0.20	0.27
2. Gondappara	38	0.02	0.22	0.20	0.28
3. Hachimanyama	14	0.02	0.14	0.11	0.20
4. Tsunasakiyama	91	0.01	0.19	0.17	0.23
5. Santonodai	16	0.06	0.31	0.23	0.41
6. Orimoto-Nishihara	93	0.02	0.21	0.20	0.26
7. Kanpukuji-Kita	15	0.02	0.20	0.18	0.24
	5	0.06	0.23	0.14	0.30

might explain these deviations from the average. At Kanpukuji-Kita, the results show two comparable Gini values, even though they were derived separately due to possible differences in excavation methods and report formats. Despite no significant change in terms of the average house size, the Gini coefficient based on house sizes slightly decreases compared to the Late Jōmon period.

The average Gini value for house area calculated for each Late Yayoi site is notably higher at 0.30 compared to the previous periods (Table 6). Among the 16 sites, 9 have Gini coefficients between 0.23 and 0.34. Some sites, such as Bukkō 仏向 (0.15) and a section at Myōjindai 明神台 (0.13), show very low Gini values, while others, such as Moritohara (0.41) and another section at Myōjindai (0.41), have high values. In contrast to the Late Jōmon period, where

Table 6 Gini coefficients for the house area at the Late Yayoi sites

	Number of pit-house	Standard error (bootstrap)	Unbiased estimator of population Gini coefficient	Bias-corrected and accelerated bootstrap 95 percent confidence interval	
				Low	High
1. Gondappara	12	0.04	0.20	0.16	0.35
2. Hachimanyama	23	0.02	0.19	0.16	0.23
3. E5	36	0.03	0.29	0.26	0.36
4. Okkoshi	21	0.05	0.34	0.28	0.44
5. Oppara	29	0.03	0.29	0.25	0.36
6. Kitagawa	23	0.05	0.40	0.35	0.52
7. Kitagawa-Omotenoue	57	0.03	0.33	0.29	0.40
8. Moritohara (excluding Y12)	18 (19)	0.06	0.41	0.34	0.52
9. Myōjindai	8	0.02	0.13	0.12	0.15
	9	0.05	0.37	0.34	0.44
	15	0.07	0.41	0.33	0.50
10. Tonoyashiki	14	0.03	0.23	0.19	0.31
	13	0.05	0.28	0.21	0.40
11. Santonodai	58	0.03	0.32	0.29	0.38
12. Terayato	29	0.03	0.34	0.30	0.42
13. Kanpukuji	44	0.03	0.35	0.31	0.44
14. Bukkō	12	0.02	0.15	0.12	0.20
15. Hiyoshidai	15	0.05	0.37	0.32	0.48
16. Kaniwa/Idaisedai	69	0.02	0.24	0.21	0.28

only a quarter of the sites had a Gini coefficient exceeding 0.3, more than half of the Late Yayoi sites exceeded this threshold, indicating an increase in Gini coefficients.

At Myōjindai and Tonoyashiki 殿屋敷, two or three Gini values were derived separately due to possible differences in excavation methods and report formats. At Myōjindai, the three Gini coefficients significantly differ. The relatively small sample sizes at some sites, such as Gondappara, Myōjindai, and Bukkō, might explain these deviations from the average. Although Kanpukuji-Kita and Kaniwa/Idaisedai 神庭・井田伊勢台 have small sample sizes of only five or six households in one set, resulting in standard error values exceeding 0.08, their larger sample sizes (38 houses for Kanpukuji-Kita and 64 houses for Kaniwa/Idaisedai) indicate that adding these smaller sets does not significantly impact the results. Thus, I combined the split samples to calculate the Gini coefficients for each site.

Although houses exceeding 100 m² were occasionally seen in the Late Jōmon and Middle Yayoi periods, the 244.1 m² of House Y32 at the Moritohara site is exceptionally high. Including this outlier in the calculation for the Moritohara site, with a sample size of 19 houses, resulted in a Gini coefficient of 0.56 with a standard error of 0.10. Excluding this outlier and recalculating with 18 houses yielded a Gini coefficient of 0.41, with the standard error reduced to 0.06. Despite the occasional existence of large houses becoming even larger, the average house size for the Late Yayoi settlements as a whole has decreased.

9 Discussion

The results of this investigation indicate that material wealth disparity in the southern Kantō region was relatively low during the Late and Final Jōmon periods (Figure 4). While Gini coefficient measurements cannot be directly equated with specific forms of social organization, the levels of disparity observed offer limited support for the Jōmon Stratified Society Theory. This theory proposes a vertically differentiated society marked by political and social distinctions rooted in factors such as division of labor and class. Since such stratification would likely be reflected in material wealth inequality, the relatively low Gini values found in this study suggest that a fully stratified society was unlikely to have existed in this region during the Late and Final Jōmon periods. Instead, the evidence appears consistent with a transitional stage of social differentiation, more in line with the characteristics of a transegalitarian society.

However, the relatively low level of wealth disparity may be specific to the study region, and the situation could differ in other areas. For comparison, I examined wealth disparity at the Kiusu site in Hokkaidō by measuring the floor area of 75 Middle and Late Jōmon pit dwellings (Table 7 and Appendix B). The results indicate a notably high level of disparity. The Gini coefficient for 46 Middle Jōmon dwellings was 0.40 with a standard error of 0.03, and for 29 Late Jōmon dwellings, it was 0.44 with a standard error of 0.04. Although Middle Jōmon houses were not analyzed in the southern Kantō dataset, the high Gini values at the Kiusu site either suggest the influence of factors other than wealth disparity on house size or point to regional variation in the development of material inequality.

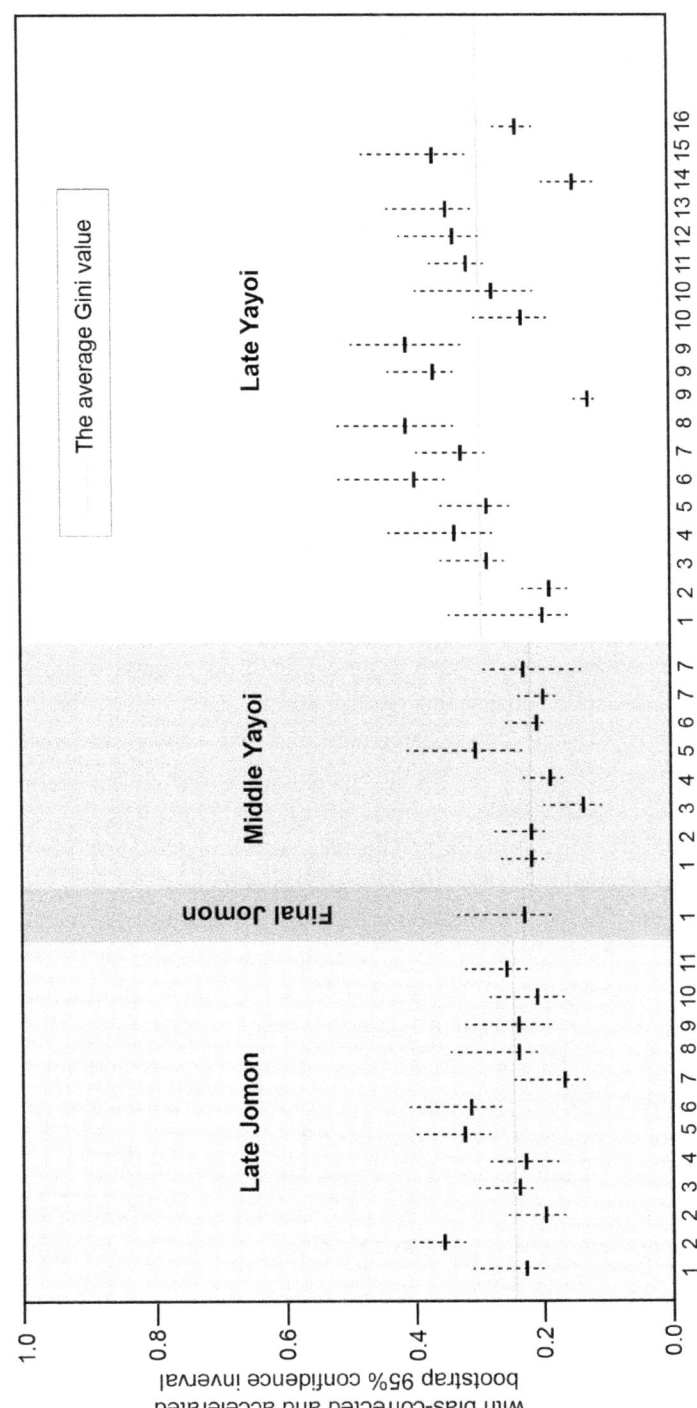

Figure 4 Gini values and bootstrapped error ranges for each period and site (See Tables 3–6 for site numbers).

Table 7 Gini coefficients for the house area at the Kiusu 5 and 7 sites

	Number of pit-house	Standard error (bootstrap)	Unbiased estimator of population Gini coefficient	Bias-corrected and accelerated bootstrap 95 percent confidence interval	
				Low	High
Kiusu 5 (Middle Jōmon)	46	0.03	0.40	0.36	0.47
Kiusu 5/7 (Late Jōmon)	29	0.04	0.44	0.38	0.53

The Gini values indicate a slight decrease in Middle Yayoi compared to Late Jōmon. The slight reduction in wealth disparity during the Middle Yayoi period in southern Kantō might be attributed to the lingering effects of catastrophic events, such as climate cooling and a significant decrease in settlements and population. Opportunities to reduce wealth inequality have sometimes been associated with catastrophic events, such as mass-mobilization warfare, transformative revolutions, state collapse, and pandemics, because violent disruptions can dismantle existing power structures and redistribute resources (Scheidel 2017; Piketty 2017). Following the continued decrease in the number of archaeological sites and the settlement hiatus after the Late Jōmon period, the return of residential areas to this region and the reconstruction of Middle Yayoi villages were accompanied by a slight decrease in wealth inequality.

In the study region, the Late Yayoi settlements exhibit a clear and noticeable increase in wealth inequality compared to the earlier periods, although variations exist between settlements. It appears that the villagers who returned to this region in the Middle Yayoi period initially constructed the village with a degree of uniformity. However, over time, as houses were modified, expanded, and rebuilt, a pattern emerged where wealthier individuals invested more in their homes. Instead of an increase in the number of large houses, some sites observed a phenomenon where a few large houses became even larger, indicating an increase in the power and wealth of their inhabitants. Conversely, the Late Yayoi period also saw a significant rise in the number of small houses.

The Lorenz curves at the Late Yayoi sites generally display a more or less proportionate deviation from the line of complete equality across the population. For instance, while the Gini value at the Kitagawa-Omotenoue 北川表の上 site

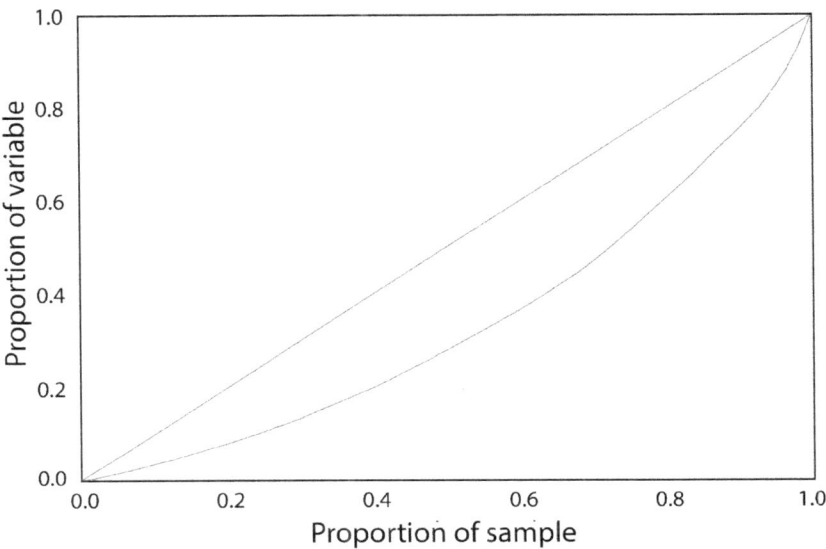

Figure 5 Lorenz curve based on house sizes at Kitagawa-Omotenoue (n = 57), showing a relatively proportional deviation from the line of perfect equality across the population.

is 0.33, the corresponding Lorenz curve indicates that the wealth difference was evenly spread across the population (Figure 5). This suggests that the wealth inequality indexed by the Gini value was continuous and not strongly associated with a specific percentile of people whose wealth level stood out significantly from the rest of the population. In other words, rather than reflecting short-term episodes of rapid wealth accumulation or loss among specific groups during the Late Yayoi period, the results suggest a more gradual broadening of wealth disparity that unfolded across several layers of the community as a whole.

When wealth disparity is visualized using a scatter plot, a clear pattern emerges across the Late Jōmon, Middle Yayoi, and Late Yayoi periods (Figure 6). Although large houses are few in number, they consistently appear in this region from the Late Jōmon period onward. Taking relative frequencies into account, it appears that slightly more large houses existed in the Late Jōmon period than in the Middle or Late Yayoi periods. In the Late Yayoi period, two exceptionally large houses appear, but these are clearly outliers and have little impact on the overall level of wealth disparity during this time. What sets Late Yayoi settlements apart from those of the Late Jōmon and Middle Yayoi periods, then, is the greater number of households living in small houses. As the scatter plot shows, more than half of the households built and maintained houses

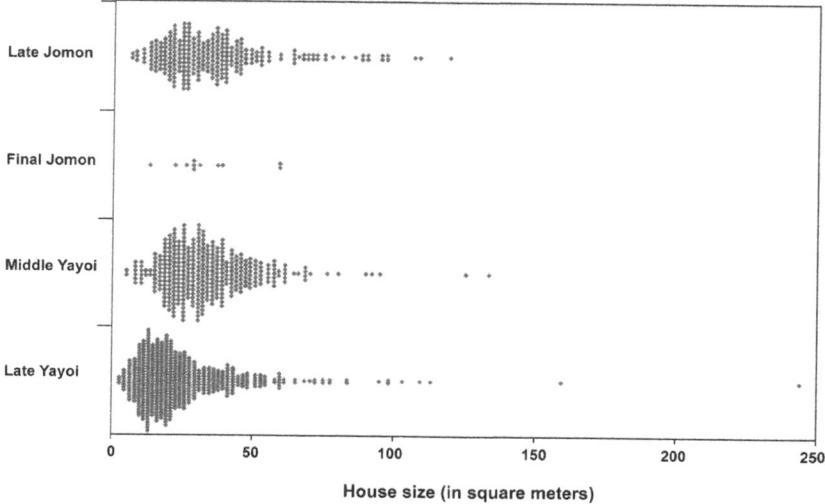

Figure 6 Scatter plot illustrating the variation in wealth disparity across the Late Jōmon, Middle Yayoi, and Late Yayoi periods.

smaller than 20 m². This rise in the proportion of small houses under 20 m² is a phenomenon not observed in earlier periods, and it significantly lowers the average house size during the Late Yayoi period. It remains unclear what kinds of people occupied these small houses and who lived in the larger ones, but regardless of the cause, such as possible land shortages, there appears to have been at least a two-tiered structure of wealth disparity between the majority of households living in smaller homes and those in larger dwellings.

The fluctuations in wealth disparity observed in this region seem to be tied to shifts in residential organization. During the Middle Yayoi period, communal regulation and more unified communities were present, whereas such structures were absent in both the preceding Late Jōmon and the subsequent Late Yayoi periods. While wealth disparity during the Late Jōmon was relatively low, it was not as low as in the Middle Yayoi period. This may be related to the characteristics of the settlement structure. According to Ishii 石井 (2011), while the number of dwellings increased during the Late Jōmon, the residential pattern remained based on highly independent small units, with each household likely managing its own storage pit. Clearly defined burial areas were also lacking, suggesting limited communal cohesion or social integration at the settlement level. Although multiple dwellings gathered in certain areas, they did not form tightly unified communities on large terraces, and the pattern of dispersed habitation continued. In such a structure composed of highly autonomous residential units, differences in household economic status would have been more visible, likely resulting in a greater degree of wealth disparity.

The marked increase in wealth disparity in this region from the late Middle to the Late Yayoi period appears also to be related to the significant changes in settlement structure and the nature of regional society. Ando 安藤 (2008a, 2008b) argues that, during the late Middle Yayoi period, relatively homogeneous and similarly sized moated settlements were scattered in this region. These settlements consciously maintained reciprocal relationships with one another, which served to suppress economic dominance by any single group and helped sustain regional social stability. Ando concludes that this kind of communal regulation can be interpreted as a response to unstable agricultural production and a high degree of dependence on external sources for essential goods, functioning effectively to curb the growth of inequality. Kuze久世 (2001) also envisions the Yayoi society in this region as taking the form of a group-oriented chiefdom. While Kuze argues that the large pit dwellings observed during the Middle Yayoi period were likely the residences of leaders such as chiefs, the near-complete absence of prestige goods in square moated graves suggests that social stratification had not been as strongly emphasized as it was in the Late Yayoi period.

During the Late Yayoi period, the population became concentrated on broad terraces with ample arable land, and large-scale settlements began to emerge. According to Ando (2008a, 2008b), while this shift allowed for flexible settlement formation based on local productivity and geography, it also marked the decline of equality among settlements. In this new social structure, certain individuals or groups emerged as stable authorities who managed the flow of goods and information and mediated instability both within and beyond the region. These central figures took on the role of addressing economic imbalances, but their presence also enabled the accumulation of wealth and power, leading to an inevitable increase in social inequality within the regional society.

Some scholars, such as Ishiwaka (2001), identify the Middle Yayoi period, not the Late Yayoi, as a time of rapid transition in the southern Kantō region. This is because a fully agricultural society was established during the mid-Middle Yayoi, and from the late Middle Yayoi onward, regional exchange involving iron tools began to develop. Even if these major social changes took place during the Middle Yayoi period, the idea that these factors contributed to wealth disparity does not necessarily contradict the timeline of increasing inequality observed in this study. For instance, the findings suggest that agrarian village life emerged in the observed settlements around or shortly before 100 BC (late Middle Yayoi), whereas significant wealth disparities did not become apparent until after the turn of the era (Late Yayoi). This time lag of

100 to 200 years may reflect the period required for wealth to accumulate gradually across generations within individual households following the adoption of an agricultural lifestyle.

Scholars support the idea that major social transformations, including the emergence of a ruling class, occurred during the Late Yayoi period. For example, although focusing on the northwestern Kantō region, Wakasa 若狭 (2022) contends that the formation of a ruling class advanced in this area toward the end of the Late Yayoi period. Environmental changes likely triggered migrations from the Tōkai region, bringing with them advanced agricultural techniques that accelerated local development. Similarly, research by Kobayashi 小林 et al. (2022) on the eastern Kantō region indicates that hierarchical settlement patterns only began to emerge during the later phase of the Late Yayoi period. By this time, populations and goods had started to concentrate in a few large hub settlements, creating disparities between these central settlements and the surrounding smaller ones. For southern Kantō, Ando (2008a: 65–71) explains that the spread of iron tools contributed to increasing wealth disparities by emphasizing the development of distribution networks for iron tools and raw materials, as well as the accompanying shifts in settlement patterns. The introduction of iron tools greatly enhanced productive capacity, while the expansion of exchange and trade networks further widened economic disparities within regional communities.

The findings of this study do not preclude the possibility that major social changes—such as the establishment of fully developed agricultural life and the emergence of networks and distribution systems for iron tools and materials—contributed to widening wealth disparities during the Late Yayoi period. Further investigation focused on southern Kantō is needed, including an examination of whether iron tools and storage spaces within dwellings were more commonly associated with larger houses, as well as other factors such as increased warfare among polities. In the same vein, the apparent narrowing of wealth disparities during the Middle Yayoi period calls for further inquiry into mechanisms that may have promoted social equality, such as communal regulation. This study, by quantifying wealth disparities through archaeological methods, reveals that inequality did not increase linearly in tandem with social complexity. Understanding what these shifts meant for the people of the time, and how they were connected to various key factors and broader social transformations, remains a critical direction for future research.

Abundant archaeological data from various parts of Japan allow for an investigation into the origins and development of economic disparity from the Late Jōmon through the Yayoi period. In particular, the reconstruction of house floor areas from numerous pit dwellings provides valuable insights. This study focuses on large-scale, extensively excavated sites in the Kōhoku area of Yokohama and the Tama region of southern Kantō. In the future, additional data will be gathered from other parts of the southern Kantō region, such as the Miura 三浦, Shonan 湘南, and Atsugi 厚木 areas, where many Jōmon and Yayoi sites have also been excavated. Ultimately, the aim is to integrate these datasets to provide a comprehensive overview of how wealth disparity evolved across the broader Kantō region.

References

Abbott, David R., Douglas B. Craig, Hannah Zanotto, Veronica X. Judd, and Brent Kober. (2021). Measuring Hohokam Household Inequality with Construction Costs of Domestic Architecture at Pueblo Grande. *American Antiquity* 86(2): 368–394.

Ames, Kenneth. (2007). The Archaeology of Rank. In *Handbook of Archaeological Theories*, edited by R. Alexander Bentley, Herbert D. G. Maschner, and Christopher Chippendale, pp. 487–513. Lanham, MD: AltaMira Press.

Ames, Kenneth and Colin Grier. (2020). Inequality on the Pacific Northwest Coast of North America Measured by House-Floor Area and Storage Capacity. *Antiquity* 94(376): 1042–1059.

Ando, Hiromichi 安藤 広道. (2008a). "Migration," "Movement," and Social Change ("Iju" "Ido" to Shakai no Henka 「移住」・「移動」と社会の変化). In *Reading the Yayoi Period from Settlements (Shuraku Kara Yomu Yayoi Jidai* 集落から読む弥生時代*)*, edited by Hiromi Shitara, Shin'ichiro Fujio, and Takehiko Matsugi, pp. 58–73. Tokyo: Doseisha.

Ando, Hiromichi. (2008b). The Hiyoshidai Site Group in Yokohama City (Yokohamashi Hiyoshidai Isekigun 横浜市日吉台遺跡群). In *New Perspectives on the Yayoi Period in Kanagawa (Shin Kanagawa/Shin Yayoiron* 新神奈川・新弥生論*)*, edited by Lecture Committee of the Kanagawa Archaeological Society 神奈川県考古学会講座担当, pp.79–88. Yokohama: Kanagawa Archaeological Society 神奈川県考古学会.

Anzai, Masahiro 安斎 正人. (2006). An Example of Stratified Society in the Jōmon Style (Jōmonshiki Kaiso Shakai no Ichijirei 縄文式階層化社会の一事例). In *Archaeology of Subsistence (Nariwai no Kokogaku* 生業の考古学*)*, edited by Tsuyoshi, Fujimoto, pp. 56–72. Tokyo: Doseisha.

Arponen, Vesa P. J., Johannes Müller, Robert Hofmann, Martin Furholt, Artur Ribeiro, Christian Horn, and Martin Hinz. (2015). Using the Capability Approach to Conceptualise Inequality in Archaeology: The Case of the Late Neolithic Bosnian Site Okolište c. 5200–4600 BCE. *Journal of Archaeological Method and Theory* 23(2): 541–560.

Augereau, Anne. (2022). In Search of the Origin of Inequalities: Gender Study and Variability of Social Organization in the First Farmers Societies of Western Europe (Linearbandkeramik culture). *Journal of Anthropological Archaeology* 66: 1–30.

Bar-Yosef, Ofer. (2001). From Sedentary Foragers to Village Hierarchies: The Emergence of Social Institutions. *Proceedings of the British Academy* 110: 1–38.

Barnard, Els. (2021). Wealth Inequality and Market Exchange: A Household-Based Approach to the Economy of Late Classic Uxul, Campeche. *Archaeological Papers of the American Anthropological Association* 32: 143–156.

Barnes, Gina L. (2019). The Jōmon–Yayoi Transition in Eastern Japan: Enquiries from the Kantō Region. *Japanese Journal of Archaeology* 7: 33–84.

Basri, Pertev and Dan Lawrence. (2020). Wealth Inequality in the Ancient Near East: A Preliminary Assessment Using Gini Coefficients and Household Size. *Cambridge Archaeological Journal* 30(4): 689–704.

Beck, Jess and Colin P. Quinn. (2022). Balancing the Scales: Archaeological Approaches to Social Inequality. *World Archaeology* 54(4): 572–583.

Black Trowel Collective (2016). *Foundations of an Anarchist Archaeology: A Community Manifesto*. https://savageminds.org/2016/10/31/foundations-of-ananarchist-archaeology-a-community-manifesto/.

Bogaard, Amy, Mattia Fochesato, and Samuel Bowles. (2019). The Farming-Inequality Nexus: New Insights from Ancient Western Eurasia. *Antiquity* 93 (371): 1129–1143.

Bogaard, Amy, Scott Ortman, Jennifer Birch, et al. (2024). The Global Dynamics of Inequality (GINI) Project: Analysing Archaeological Housing Data. *Antiquity* 98(397): 1–7.

Bogaard, Amy, Amy Styring, Jade Whitlam, Mattia Fochesato, and Samuel Bowles. (2018). Farming, Inequality, and Urbanization: A Comparative Analysis of Late Prehistoric Northern Mesopotamia and Southwestern Germany. In *Ten Thousand Years of Inequality: The Archaeology of Wealth Differences*, edited by Timothy A. Kohler and Michael E. Smith, pp. 201–229. Tucson: University of Arizona Press.

Borck, Lewis and Matthew C. Sanger. (2017). An Introduction to Anarchism and Archaeology. *The SAA Archaeological Record* 17(1): 9–16.

Borgerhoff Mulder, Monique, Samuel Bowles, Tom Hertz, et al. (2009). Intergenerational Wealth Transmission and the Dynamics of Inequality in Small-Scale Societies. *Science* 326: 682–688.

Bowles, Samuel, Eric Alden Smith, and Monique Borgerhoff Mulder. (2010). The Emergence and Persistence of Inequality in Premodern Societies: Introduction to the Special Section. *Current Anthropology* 51(1): 7–17.

Chase, Adrian S. Z. (2017). Residential Inequality among the Ancient Maya: Operationalizing Household Architectural Volume at Caracol, Belize. *Research Reports in Belizean Archaeology* 14: 31–39.

Chesson, Meredith S. and Nathan Goodale. (2014). Population Aggregation, Residential Storage and Socioeconomic Inequality at Early Bronze Age Numayra, Jordan. *Journal of Anthropological Archaeology* 35: 117–134.

City of Yokohama, Policy Bureau, General Affairs Division (2020). *2018 Housing and Land Survey: Basic Tabulation on Housing and Households, Table 44–4: Number of households by annual income class (9 categories), household type (2 categories), and housing ownership status (5 categories); average number of persons, rooms, and tatami mats per household.* Accessed July 8, 2025. https://share.google/z8ga5DmMhHqd5bZGW.

Coupland, Gary, David Bilton, Terence Clark, et al. (2016). A Wealth of Beads: Evidence for Material Wealth-Based Inequality in the Salish Sea Region, 4000–3500 Cal B.P. *American Antiquity* 81(2): 294–315.

Crawford, Gary W. (2011). Advances in Understanding Early Agriculture in Japan. *Current Anthropology* 52(4):1–15.

Dennehy, Timothy J., Benjamin W. Stanley, and Michael E. Smith. (2016). Social Inequality and Access to Services in Premodern Cities. *Archaeological Papers of the American Anthropological Association* 27: 143–160.

Fargher Lane F., Ricardo R. Antorcha-Pedemonte, Verenice Y. Heredia Espinoza, et al. (2020). Wealth Inequality, Social Stratification, and the Built Environment in Late Prehispanic Highland Mexico: A Comparative Analysis with Special Emphasis on Tlaxcallan. *Journal of Anthropological Archaeology* 58: 1–17.

Flad, Rowan K. (2002). Ritual or Structure? Analysis of Burial Elaboration at Dadianzi, Inner Mongolia. *Journal of East Asian Archaeology* 3(3–4): 23–52.

Flannery, Kent and Joyce Marcus. (2012). *The Creation of Inequality: How Our Prehistoric Ancestors Set the Stage for Monarchy, Slavery, and Empire.* Cambridge: Harvard University Press.

Flexner, James L. and Edward Gonzalez-Tennant. (2018). Anarchy and Archaeology. *Journal of Contemporary Archaeology* 5(2): 213–219.

Fochesato, Mattia, Amy Bogaard, and Samuel Bowles. (2019). Comparing Ancient Inequalities: The Challenges of Comparability, Bias and Precision. *Antiquity* 93(370): 853–869.

Gibbons, Ann. (2019). Bronze Age Inequality and Family Life Revealed in Powerful Study: Combined Methods Show Women Married Far from Home. *Science* 366(6462): 168.

González-Ruibal, Alfredo. (2025). Traditions of Equality: The Archaeology of Egalitarianism and Egalitarian Behavior in Sub-Saharan Africa (First and Second Millennium CE). *Journal of Archaeological Method and Theory* 32 (6):1–49.

Graeber, David and David Wengrow. (2021). *The Dawn of Everything: A New History of Humanity*. New York: Farrar, Straus and Giroux.

Green, Adams S. (2021). Killing the Priest-King: Addressing Egalitarianism in the Indus Civilization. *Journal of Archaeological Research* 29: 153–202.

Green, Adam S., Toby C. Wilkinson, Darryl Wilkinson, Nancy Highcock and Thomas P. Leppard. (2023). *Cities and Citadels: An Archaeology of Inequality and Economic Growth*. New York: Routledge.

Gurven, Michael, Monique Borgerhoff Mulder, Paul L. Hooper, et al. (2010). Domestication Alone Does Not Lead to Inequality. *Current Anthropology* 51 (1): 49–64.

Hayashi, Kensaku 林 謙作. (2001). Was Jōmon Society a Stratified Society? (Jōmon Shakai wa Kaiso Shakai ka 縄文社会は階層社会か). In *Archaeology of Jōmon Society* 縄文社会の考古学, pp. 536–552. Tokyo: Doseisha.

Hayden, Brian and Emmanuel Guy. (2024). Paleo Storage, Paleo Surplus, and Paleo Inequality in the Périgord. *Journal of Archaeological Method and Theory* 31:1771–1801.

Hudson, Mark J., Ilona R. Bausch, Martine Robbeets, et al. (2021). Bronze Age Globalisation and Eurasian Impacts on Later Jōmon Social Change. *Journal of World Prehistory* 34: 121–158.

Hutson, Scott. (2016). The Spatial Experience of Inequality. In *The Ancient Urban Maya: Neighborhoods, Inequality, and Built Form*, pp. 139–169. Gainesville: University Press of Florida.

Hutson, Scott R., Timothy S. Hare, Travis W. Stanton, et al. (2021). A Space of One's Own: Houselot Size among the Ancient Maya. *Journal of Anthropological Archaeology* 64: 1–15.

Ishii, Hiroshi 石井寛. (2011). Twenty Years of Excavation Work in the Kōhoku New Town Area (Kōhoku N.T. Chiiki no Seiri Sagyo 20-nen 港北N.T.地域の整理作業20年). In *Archaeological Seminar: Recent Trends in Kanagawa Archaeology (Kokogaku Koza Kanagawa no Kokogaku/Saikin no Doko* 考古学講座神奈川の考古学・最近の動向), pp. 5–10. Yokohama: Kanagawa Archaeological Association 神奈川県考古学会.

Ishii, Hiroshi 石井 寛. (1994). A Preliminary Study on the Composition of Late Jōmon Settlements (Jōmonkoki Shuraku no Kosei ni Kansuru Ichishiron 縄文後期集落の構成に関する一試論). *Journal of Jōmon Period Studies* 縄文時代 5: 77–110.

Ishikawa, Hideshi 石川日出志. (2022). The Nakazato Site and the Spread of Agriculture in the Southern Kantō Region (Nakazato Iseki to Minami Kantō Chiho no Nokoka 中里遺跡と南関東地方の農耕化). In *Yayoi Culture in Southern Kantō: Interaction with East Asia and the Development of*

Agriculture (Minami Kantō no Yayoi Bunka: Higashi Ajia tono Koryu to Nokoryoku 南関東の弥生文化: 東アジアとの交流と農耕力*)*, edited by Tomoko Nagatomo, Hideshi Ishikawa, and Yoshiki Fukazawa, pp. 58–73. Tokyo: Yoshikawa Kōbunkan 吉川弘文館.

Ishikawa, Hideshi 石川 日出志. (2001). Drastic Social Change in First Century B.C. Kantō, Eastern Japan (Kantōchiho Yayoi Jidai Chukichuyo no Shakai Hendo 関東地方弥生時代中期中葉の社会変動). *Sundai Historical Review* 駿台史学 113: 57–94.

Jörgensen, Lars. (1988). Family Burial Practices and Inheritance Systems: The Development of an Iron Age Society from 500 BC–AD 1000 on Bornholm, Denmark. *Acta Archaeologica* 58: 17–53.

Kanagawa Archaeological Society 神奈川県考古学会. (2011). *Archaeology in Kanagawa: Recent Trends (Kanagawa no Kokogaku: Saikin no Doko* 神奈川の考古学・最近の動向*)*. Yokohama: Kanagawa Archaeological Society.

Kaneko, Akihiko 金子 昭彦. (2005). Transegalitarian Society and the Mortuary System of the Kamegaoka Culture (Kaisoka Shakai to Kamegaoka Bunka no Haka 階層化社会と亀ヶ岡文化の墓). *Journal of the Japanese Archaeological Association* 日本考古学 12(19): 1–28.

Kanpukuji-Kita Site Excavation Team 観福寺北遺跡発掘調査団. (1997). *Kanpukuji-Kita Site Group, Sekikōchi Site Excavation Report (Kanpukuji-Kita Isekigun Sekikōchi Iseki Hakkutsu Chosa Hokokusho* 観福寺北遺跡群関耕地遺跡発掘調査報告書*)*. Yokohama: Kanpukuji-Kita Site Excavation Team.

Kay, Kevin, Scott Haddow, Christopher Knüsel, et al. (2023). No Gentry but Grave-Makers: Inequality beyond Property Accumulation at Neolithic Çatalhöyük. World Archaeology 54(4): 584–601.

Killewald, Alexandra, Fabian T. Pfeffer, and Jared N. Schachner. (2017). Wealth Inequality and Accumulation. *Annual Review of Sociology* 43: 379–404.

Kim, Minkoo. (2025). Intragroup Social Differentiation and Household Inequality in Prehistoric Mumun Settlements of Korea. *Journal of Anthropological Archaeology* 78: 1–14.

Klinkenberg, Victor and Bleda S. Düring. (2023). Inequality before the Bronze Age: The Case of Chalcolithic Cyprus. *Oxford Journal of Archaeology* 42(1): 2–16.

Kobayashi, Ken'ichi 小林謙一, Shin'ichiro Fujio 藤尾慎一郎, and Takehiko Matsugi 松木武彦. (2020). Chronology and Periodization of Prehistoric Japan (Jōmon, Yayoi, and Kofun Periods) (Senji Jidai (Jōmon, Yayoi, Kofun) no Nendai to Jidai Kubun 先史時代(縄文・弥生・古墳)の年代と時代区分). In *Rethinking Japanese History Through Climate Change, Vol. 3*

(*Kikohendo kara Minaosu Nihonshi* 気候変動から読みなおす日本史 3), edited by Takeshi Nakatsuka, Kunihiko Wakabayashi, and Noboru Higami, pp. 35–59. Kyoto: Rinsen Shoten.

Kobayashi, Seiji 小林 青樹, Naoyuki Todoroki 轟 直行, and Kazuyuki Ikeda 池田 和之. (2022). Middle to Late Yayoi Period Society in Eastern Kantō Area (Tobu Kantōchiiki ni Okeru Yayoi Chukoki Shakai 東部関東地域における弥生中後期社会). *Bulletin of the National Museum of Japanese History* 国立歴史民俗博物館研究報告 231: 11–43.

Kobayashi, Tatsuo 小林 達雄. (2000). Villages, Society, and Worldview in the Jōmon Period (Jōmon Jidai no Mura to Shakai to Sekaikan 縄文時代のムラと社会と世界観). In *Revisiting Japanese Archaeology (Nihon Kokogaku wo Minaosu* 日本考古学を見直す*)*, edited by the Japanese Archaeological Association, pp. 101–124. Tokyo: Gakuseisha.

Kohler, Timothy A., and Rebecca Higgins. (2016). Quantifying Household Inequality in Early Pueblo Villages. *Current Anthropology* 57: 690–697.

Kohler, Timothy A., and Michael E. Smith. (2018). *Ten Thousand Years of Inequality: The Archaeology of Wealth Differences*. Tucson: University of Arizona Press.

Kohler, Timothy A., Michael E. Smith, Amy Bogaard, et al. (2017). Greater Post-Neolithic Wealth Disparities in Eurasia than in North America and Mesoamerica. *Nature* 551: 619–622.

Kuijt, Ian. (2024). Reconsidering Narratives of Household Social Inequality. *Journal of Anthropological Archaeology* 75: 1–4.

Kunikita, Dai 國木田 大. (2023). Climate Change and the Late Jōmon Period (Kiko Hendo to Jōmon Banki 気候変動と縄文晩期). *Archaeology Quarterly* 季刊考古学 Supplement 40: 147–150.

Kuze, Tatsuo 久世辰男. (2001). *Yayoi Society in Southern Kantō* 南関東の弥生社会. Tokyo: Rokuichi Shobo 六一書房.

LaMotta, Vincent M. and Schiffer, Michael B. (1999). Formation Processes of House Floor Assemblages. In *the Archaeology of Household Activities*, edited by Penelope M. Allison, pp. 19–29. London: Routledge.

Matsugi, Takehiko 松木 武彦. (1995). Towards a Comprehensive Explanation of Warfare and Social Evolution in Protohistoric Japan (Yayoi Jidai no Senso to Nihon Retto Shakai no Hatten Katei 弥生時代の戦争と日本列島社会の発展過程). *Quarterly of Archaeological Studies* 考古学研究 42(3): 33–47.

Matsugi, Takehiko 松木 武彦. (1996). State Formation in the Japanese Archipelago (Nihon Retto no Kokka Keisei 日本列島の国家形成). In *Formation of States (Kokka no Keisei* 国家の形成*)*, edited by Takeshi Ueki, pp. 233–276. Tokyo: San'ichi Shobo.

Matsugi, Takehiko 松木 武彦. (2007) *War and Early State Formation in the Japanese Archipelago (Nihon Retto no Senso to Shoki Kokka Keisei* 日本列島の戦争と初期国家形成*)*. Tokyo: University of Tokyo Press.

Mattison, Siobhán M. Mattison, Eric A. Smith, Mary K. Shenk, and Ethan E. Cochrane. (2016). The Evolution of Inequality. *Evolutionary Anthropology* 25: 184–199.

McCoy, Mark D., and Joseph L. Panuska. (2024). Visible Wealth in Past Societies: A Case Study of Domestic Architecture from the Hawaiian Islands. *Cambridge Archaeological Journal* 34(3): 373–383.

Mittnik, Alissa, Ken Massy, Corina Knipper, et al. (2019). Kinship-Based Social Inequality in Bronze Age Europe. *Science* 366: 731–734.

Miyamoto, Kazuo 宮本一夫. (2018). A Reconsideration of the Absolute Chronology for the Beginning of the Yayoi Period (Yayoi Jidai Kaishiki no Jitsunendai Sairon 弥生時期開始期の実年代再論). *Kōkogaku Zasshi* 考古学雑誌 100(2): 1–27.

Morehart, Christopher T., and Kristin De Lucia. (2015). *Surplus: The Politics of Production and the Strategies of Everyday Life*. Boulder: University Press of Colorado.

Munson, Jessica and Jonathan Scholnick. (2022). Wealth and Well-being in an Ancient Maya Community: A Framework for Studying the Quality of Life in Past Societies. *Journal of Archaeological Method and Theory* 29: 1–30.

Murakami, Yasuyuki 村上 恭通. (2007). *The Process of Ancient State Formation and Iron Production (Kodai Kokka Seiritsu Katei to Tekki Seisan* 古代国家成立過程と鉄器生産*)*. Tokyo: Aoki Shoten.

Nagatomo, Tomoko 長友朋子, Hideshi Ishikawa 石川日出志, and Yoshiki Fukazawa 深澤芳樹 (eds). (2022). *Yayoi Culture in Southern Kantō: Interaction with East Asia and the Development of Agriculture (Minami Kantō no Yayoi Bunka: Higashi Ajia tono Koryu to Nokoryoku* 南関東の弥生文化: 東アジアとの交流と農耕力*)*. Tokyo: Yoshikawa Kōbunkan 吉川弘文館.

Negita, Yoshio 禰宜田 佳男. (2019). *The Formation of Agricultural Culture and the Yayoi Society in Kinki (Nokobunka no Keisei to Kinki Yayoi Shakai* 農耕文化の形成と近畿弥生社会*)*. Tokyo: Doseisha.

Nakamura, Okiz 中村 大. (1999). Reading the Stratification of Jōmon Society through Burial Practices (Bosei Kara Yomu Jōmon Shakai no Kaisoka 墓制から読む縄文社会の階層化). In *The World of Latest Jōmon Studies (Saishin Jōmongaku no Sekai* 最新縄文学の世界*)*, edited by Tasuo Kobayashi, pp. 48–60. Tokyo: Asahi Shinbunsha.

Nishimura, Yoko. (2023). Domestic Material Culture and Wealth Equality: Bronze Age Houses and Intramural Tombs at Titriş Höyük, Turkey. *Near Eastern Archaeology* 86(3): 176–184.

Nishimura, Yoko. (2025). Centralized Urban Planning and Economic Segregation: Wealth Inequality in Tell Asmar and Khafajah, Mesopotamia. *Iraq* 86: 297–318.

Noxon, Corey Tyler. (2025). A Paleodemographic Approach to the Middle Jōmon Boom and Bust Population Pattern. *Japanese Journal of Archaeology* 12: 2–30.

Olson, Jan M. and Michael E. Smith. (2016). Material Expressions of Wealth and Social Class at Aztec-Period Sites in Morelos, Mexico. *Ancient Mesoamerica* 27: 133–147.

Oravkinová, Dominika and Jozef Vladár. (2020). Some Are More Equal Than Others: Intrasettlement Social Organization in Spišský Štvrtok (EBA/MBA, Slovakia). *Cambridge Archaeological Journal* 31(2): 183–210.

Osterholtz, Anna J. and Ivan Valent. (2025). The Taphonomy of Status: The Creation of Group Identity and Social Inequality in Medieval Croatia. *Journal of Archaeological Method and Theory* 32: 1–27.

Pailes, Matthew. (2014). Social Network Analysis of Early Classic Hohokam Corporate Group Inequality. *American Antiquity* 79(3): 465–486.

Panitz-Cohen, Nava. (2011). A Tale of Two Houses: The Role of Pottery in Reconstructing Household Wealth and Composition. In *Household Archaeology in Ancient Israel and Beyond*, edited by Assaf Yasur-Landau, Jennie R. Ebeling, and Laura B. Mazow, pp. 85–105. Boston: Brill.

Pearson, Richard. (2007). Debating Jōmon Social Complexity. *Asian Perspectives* 46(2): 361–388.

Piketty, Thomas (translated by Arthur Goldhammer). (2017). *Capital in the Twenty-First Century*. Cambridge: Harvard University Press.

Politopoulos, Aris, Catherine J. Frieman, James L. Flexner, and Lewis Borck. (2024). An Anarchist Archaeology of Equality: Pasts and Futures Against Hierarchy. *Cambridge Archaeological Journal* 34(4): 531–545.

Porčić, Marko. (2019). Evaluating Social Complexity and Inequality in the Balkans between 6500 and 4200 BC. *Journal of Archaeological Research* 27: 335–390.

Prentiss, Anna Marie, Thomas A. Foor, Ashley Hampton, Ethan Ryan, and Matthew J. Walsh. (2018). The Evolution of Material Wealth-Based Inequality: The Record of Housepit 54, Bridge River, British Columbia. *American Antiquity* 83(4): 598–618.

Price, T. Douglas and Gary M. Feinman. (1995). *Foundations of Social Inequality*. New York: Plenum Press.

Price, T. Douglas and Gary M. Feinman. (2010). *Pathways to Power: New Perspectives on the Emergence of Social Inequality*. New York: Springer.

Rakopoulos, Theodoros and Knut Rio. (2018). Introduction to an Anthropology of Wealth. *History and Anthropology* 29(3): 275–291.

Saeki, Arikiyo. (2018). *Treatise on the People of Wa in the Chronicle of the Kingdom of Wei: The World's Earliest Written Text on Japan*, translated by Joshua A. Fogel. Portland: MerwinAsia.

Sakaguchi, Takashi 坂口 隆. (2011). Mortuary Variability and Status Differentiation in the Late Jōmon of Hokkaido Based on the Analysis of Shuteibo (Communal Cemeteries). *Journal of World Prehistory* 24: 275–308.

Sasaki, Fujio 佐々木 藤雄. (2002). Stone Circles and Jōmon Stratified Society (Kanjo Resseki to Jōmon Shiki Kaiso Shakai 環状列石と縄文式階層社会). In *Jōmon Social Theory (Jōmon Shakairon 縄文社会論)* Volume 2, pp. 3–50. Tokyo: Doseisha.

Scheidel, Walter. (2017). *The Great Leveler: Violence and the History of Inequality from the Stone Age to the Twenty-First Century*. Princeton: Princeton University Press.

Schneider, Harold. (1974). *Economic Man: The Anthropology of Economics*. New York: Free Press.

Schroder, Whittaker, Timothy Murtha, Charles Golden, et al. (2023). Regional Household Variation and Inequality across the Maya Landscape. *Journal of Anthropological Archaeology* 72: 1–19.

Semple, Sarah and Rui Gomes Coelho. (2022). Materialising Inequalities in Past, Present and Future. *World Archaeology* 54(4): 493–501.

Shenk, Mary K., Monique Borgerhoff Mulder, Jan Beise, et al. (2010). Intergenerational Wealth Transmission among Agriculturalists: Foundations of Agrarian Inequality. *Current Anthropology* 51(1): 65–83.

Shitara, Hiromi 設楽 博己. (2004). A Background to Reburial (Saiso no Haikei 再葬の背景). *Bulletin of the National Museum of Japanese History* 国立歴史民俗博物館研究報告 12: 357–380.

Shitara, Hiromi 設楽 博己. (2014). *Jōmon Society and Yayoi Society (Jōmon Shakai to Yayoi Shakai 縄文社会と弥生社会)*. Tokyo: Keibunsha.

Shitara, Hiromi 設楽 博己. (2017). *Formation of Yayoi Culture (Yayoi Bunka Keiseiron 弥生文化形成論)*. Tokyo: Hanawa Shobo.

Shitara, Hiromi 設楽 博己. (2022). *Jōmon vs. Yayoi: Comparing Prehistoric Periods from Nine Perspectives (Jōmon Tai Yayoi: Senshi Jidai wo Kokonotsu no Tende Hikakusuru 縄文vs.弥生：先史時代を九つの視点で比較する)*. Tokyo: Chikuma Shobo.

Simelius, Samuli. (2023). Unequal Housing in Pompeii: Using House Size to Measure Inequality. *World Archaeology* 54(4): 602–624.

Siteleki, Mncedisi J., and Per Ditlef Fredriksen. (2024). Inequality or Insecurity? The Case of Pre-Colonial Farming Communities in Southern Africa. *Antiquity* 98(397): 135–154.

Smith, Eric Alden, Monique Borgerhoff Mulder, Samuel Bowles, et al. (2010). Production Systems, Inheritance, and Inequality in Premodern Societies. *Current Anthropology* 51(1): 85–94.

Smith, Michael E. (1987). Household Possessions and Wealth in Agrarian States: Implications for Archaeology. *Journal of Anthropological Archaeology* 6: 297–335.

Smith, Michael E. (2021). Durable Inequality in Aztec Society. *Journal of Anthropological Research* 77(2): 162–186.

Smith, Michael E., Timothy Dennehy, April Kamp-Whittaker, Emily Colon, and Rebecca Harkness. (2014). Quantitative Measures of Wealth Inequality in Ancient Central Mexican Communities. *Advances in Archaeological Practice* 2: 311–323.

Squitieri, Andrea and Mark Altaweel. (2022). Empires and the Acceleration of Wealth Inequality in the Pre-Islamic near East: An Archaeological Approach. *Archaeological and Anthropological Sciences* 14: 1–16.

Stone, Elizabeth C. (2018). The Trajectory of Society Inequality in Ancient Mesopotamia. In *Ten Thousand Years of Inequality: The Archaeology of Wealth Differences*, edited by Timothy A. Kohler and Michael E. Smith, pp. 230–261. Tucson: University of Arizona Press.

Strawinska-Zanko, Urszula, Larry S. Liebovitch, April Watson, and Clifford T. Brown. (2018). Capital in the First Century: The Evolution of Inequality in Ancient Maya Society. In *Mathematical Modeling of Social Relationships*, edited by Urszula Strawinska-Zanko and Larry S. Liebovitch, pp. 161–192. Cham, Switzerland: Springer.

Takahashi, Ken 高橋　健. (2024). *The Structure of Yayoi Period Villages in Southern Kantō: The Ōtsuka and Saikachido Sites (Minami Kantō/Yayoi Jidai no Mura no Sugata: Otsuka/Saikachido Iseki* 南関東・弥生時代のムラの姿: 大塚・歳勝土遺跡*)*. Tokyo: Shinsensha 新泉社.

Takahashi, Ryuzaburo 高橋 寵三郎. (2001). Some Considerations on Social Complexity and Stratification in Late/Final Jōmon Society (Jōmon Kobanki no Fukugoka to Kaisoka Katei wo Do Toraeruka 縄文後・晩期社会の複合化と階層化過程をどう捉えるか). *Bulletin of the Graduate Division of Literature of Waseda University* 早稲田大学大学院文学研究科紀要 47: 61–75.

Takaku, Kenji 高久 健二. (2011). Relations with Lelang and Daifang Commanderies (Rakuro, Taihogun tono Kankei 楽浪・帯方郡との関係). In *The Beginnings of the Kofun Period (Kofun Jidai eno Taido* 古墳時代へ

の胎動), edited by Hiromi Shitara, Shin'ichiro Fujio, and Takehiko Matsugi, pp. 39–53. Tokyo: Doseisha.

Tanabe, Eri 田邊 えり. (2023). Kantō Region: The Rise and Fall of the Angyo Culture (Kantō Chiho: Angyo Bunka no Seisui 関東地方: 安行文化の盛衰). *Archaeology Quarterly* 季刊考古学 Supplement 40: 27–30.

Thompson, Amy E., Gary M. Feinman, and Keith M. Prufer. (2021). Assessing Classic Maya Multi-Scalar Household Inequality in Southern Belize. *PLoS ONE* 16(3): 1–30.

Vésteinsson, Orri, Michelle Hegmon, Jette Arneborg, Glen Rice, and Will G. Russell. (2019). Dimensions of Inequality. Comparing the North Atlantic and the US Southwest. *Journal of Anthropological Archaeology* 54: 172–191.

Vila, Eduardo Vijande, Salvador Domínguez-Bella, Juan Jesús Cantillo Duarte, Javier Martínez López, and Antonio Barrena Tocino. (2015). Social Inequalities in the Neolithic of Southern Europe: The Grave Goods of the Campo de Hockey Necropolis (San Fernando, Cádiz, Spain). *Comptes Rendus Palevol* 14: 147–161.

Wakasa, Toru 若狭 徹. (2022). Archaeological Site Dynamics and Environmental Changes in the Late Yayoi Period in the Northwestern Kantō Region (Hokusei Kantō ni Okeru Yayoi Koki no Iseki Dotai to Kankyo Hendo 北西関東における弥生後期の遺跡動態と環境変動). *Bulletin of the National Museum of Japanese History* 国立歴史民俗博物館研究報告 231: 45–69.

Watanabe, Hitoshi 渡辺 仁. (1990). *Jōmon Stratified Society (Jōmonshiki Kaisoka Shakai* 縄文式階層化社会). Tokyo: Rokko Publishing.

Wengrow, David, Brenna Hassett, Haluk Sağlamtimur, et al. (2025). Inequality at the Dawn of the Bronze Age: The Case of Başur Höyük, a 'Royal' Cemetery at the Margins of the Mesopotamian World. *Cambridge Archaeological Journal* 34: 293–304.

Wilkinson, Darryl. (2019). Infrastructure and Inequality: An Archaeology of the Inka Road through the Amaybamba Cloud Forests. *Journal of Social Archaeology* 19(1): 27–46.

Windler, Arne, Rainer Thiele, and Johannes Müller. (2013). Increasing Inequality in Chalcolithic Southeast Europe: The Case of Durankulak. *Journal of Archaeological Science* 40: 204–210.

Wright, Katherine I. (2014). Domestication and Inequality? Households, Corporate Groups and Food Processing Tools at Neolithic Çatalhöyük. *Journal of Anthropological Archaeology* 33: 1–33.

Yamada, Yasuhiro 山田 康弘. (2020). The History of Archaeology and Its Social Background (Kokogakushi to Shakai Haikei 考古学史と社会背景). *Archaeology Quarterly* 季刊考古学 150: 28–33.

Yamamoto, Teruhisa 山本 暉久. (2005). Prospects of Stratified Society Theory in the Jōmon Period (Jōmon Jidai Kaisoka Shakairon no Yukue 縄文時代階層化社会論の行方). *Journal of Jōmon Period Studies* 縄文時代 16: 111–142.

Yayoi Period Research Project Team 弥生時代研究プロジェクトチーム. (2011). Yayoi Period Metal Artifacts Unearthed in Kanagawa Prefecture 3 (Kanagawa-ken Shutsudo no Yayoi Jidai Kinzokuki 神奈川県内出土の弥生時代金属器3). *Kanagawa Research Bulletin* かながわ研究紀要16: 25–36.

Yokohama City Buried Cultural Property Center 横浜市埋蔵文化財センター. (1991). *Otsuka Site: Excavation Report of Yayoi Period Moated Settlement Sites 1, Structures Section (Otsuka Iseki: Yayoi Jidai Kango Shurakuato no Hakkutsu Chosa Hokoku 1, Ikohen* 大塚遺跡: 弥生時代環濠集落址の発掘調査報告1遺構編*)*. Report on the Excavation of Buried Cultural Properties in the Kōhoku New Town Area 港北ニュータウン地域内埋蔵文化財調査報告 12. Yokohama: Yokohama City Buried Cultural Property Center.

Yokohama City Buried Cultural Property Investigation Committee 横浜市埋蔵文化財調査委員会. (1980). *Orimoto-Nishihara Site (Orimoto-Nishihara Iseki* 折本西原遺跡*)*. Yokohama: Yokohama City Buried Cultural Property Investigation Committee.

Yokohama City Historical Foundation Buried Cultural Property Center 横浜市ふるさと歴史財団. (2008). *Keshōdai Site (Keshōdai Iseki* 華蔵台遺跡*)* Volume 2. Report on the Excavation of Buried Cultural Properties in the Kōhoku New Town Area 港北ニュータウン地域内埋蔵文化財調査報告 41. Yokohama: Yokohama City Historical Foundation.

Yokohama City Historical Foundation Buried Cultural Property Center 横浜市ふるさと歴史財団. (2009). *Kitagawaomote-no-Ue Site (Kitagawaomote-no-Ue Iseki* 北川表の上遺跡*)*. Report on the Excavation of Buried Cultural Properties in the Kōhoku New Town Area 港北ニュータウン地域内埋蔵文化財調査報告 42. Yokohama: Yokohama City Historical Foundation.

Yokohama City Historical Foundation Buried Cultural Property Center 横浜市ふるさと歴史財団. (2011). *Oppara Site (Oppara Iseki* 大原遺跡*)*. Report on the Excavation of Buried Cultural Properties in the Kōhoku New Town Area 港北ニュータウン地域内埋蔵文化財調査報告 44. Yokohama: Yokohama City Board of Education.

Yokohama City Historical Foundation Buried Cultural Property Center 横浜市ふるさと歴史財団. (2017). *Gondappara Site II (Gondappara Iseki* 権田原遺跡 2*)*. Report on the Excavation of Buried Cultural Properties in the Kōhoku New Town Area 港北ニュータウン地域内埋蔵文化財調査報告

49. Yokohama: Yokohama City Board of Education and Yokohama City Historical Foundation.

Yu, Shi-Yong, Xue-Xiang Chen, and Hui Fang. (2019). Inferring Inequality in Prehistoric Societies from Grave Sizes: A Methodological Framework. *Archaeological and Anthropological Sciences* 11: 4947–4958.

References for House Area Data from the Archaeological Sites

Azuma Archaeological Institute 吾妻考古学研究所. (2007). *Shinohara-Ōhara-Kita Site (Shinohara-Ōhara-Kita Iseki* 篠原大原北遺跡*)*. Tokyo: Nomura Real Estate.

Department of Ethnology and Archaeology of Keio University 慶應義塾大学文学部民族学考古学研究室. (2019). *Hiyoshidai Site Group Excavation Report (Hiyoshidai Isekigun Hakkutsu Chosa Hokokusho* 日吉台遺跡群発掘調査報告書*)*. Tokyo: Department of Ethnology and Archaeology of Keio University.

Department of History, College of Humanities and Sciences of Nihon University 日本大学文理学部史学研究室. (1977). *Ida-Iseidai Site Excavation Report, Nakahara Ward, Kawasaki City (Kawasakishi Nakaharaku Ida-Isedai Iseki Hakkutsu Chosa Hokokusho* 川崎市中原区 井田伊勢台遺跡発掘調査報告書*)*. Tokyo: Department of History, College of Humanities and Sciences of Nihon University.

Hokkaidō Buried Cultural Property Center 北海道埋蔵文化財センター. (1996). *Kiusu 7 Site (Kiusu 7 Iseki* キウス7遺跡*)*. Hokkaidō Buried Cultural Property Center Investigation Report 北海道埋蔵文化財センター調査報告書 105. Hokkaidō: Hokkaidō Buried Cultural Property Center.

Hokkaidō Buried Cultural Property Center 北海道埋蔵文化財センター. (1997). *Kiusu 5 Site (Kiusu 5 Iseki* キウス5遺跡*)*. Hokkaidō Buried Cultural Property Center Investigation Report 北海道埋蔵文化財センター調査報告書 115. Hokkaidō: Hokkaidō Buried Cultural Property Center.

Hokkaidō Buried Cultural Property Center 北海道埋蔵文化財センター. (1997). *Kiusu 5 Site (Kiusu 5 Iseki* キウス5遺跡*)*. Hokkaidō Buried Cultural Property Center Investigation Report 北海道埋蔵文化財センター調査報告書 116. Hokkaidō: Hokkaidō Buried Cultural Property Center.

Hokkaidō Buried Cultural Property Center 北海道埋蔵文化財センター. (1997). *Kiusu 7 Site (Kiusu 7 Iseki* キウス7遺跡*)*. Hokkaidō Buried Cultural Property Center Investigation Report 北海道埋蔵文化財セン

ター調査報告書 117. Hokkaidō: Hokkaidō Buried Cultural Property Center.

Hokkaidō Buried Cultural Property Center 北海道埋蔵文化財センター. (1998). *Kiusu 5 Site (Kiusu 5 Iseki* キウス5遺跡*)*. Hokkaidō Buried Cultural Property Center Investigation Report 北海道埋蔵文化財センター調査報告書 125. Hokkaidō: Hokkaidō Buried Cultural Property Center.

Hokkaidō Buried Cultural Property Center 北海道埋蔵文化財センター. (1998). *Kiusu 7 Site (Kiusu 7 Iseki* キウス7遺跡*)*. Hokkaidō Buried Cultural Property Center Investigation Report 北海道埋蔵文化財センター調査報告書 127. Hokkaidō: Hokkaidō Buried Cultural Property Center.

Hokkaidō Buried Cultural Property Center 北海道埋蔵文化財センター. (2013). *Kiusu 5 Site (Kiusu 5 Iseki*キウス5遺跡*)*. Hokkaidō Buried Cultural Property Center Investigation Report 北海道埋蔵文化財センター調査報告書299. Hokkaidō: Hokkaidō Buried Cultural Property Center.

Kanagawa Archaeological Foundation かながわ考古学財団. (2004). *Shinohara-Ōhara Site (Shinohara-Ōhara Iseki* 篠原大原遺跡*)*. Kanagawa Archaeological Foundation Investigation Report かながわ考古学財団調査報告 175. Yokohama: Kanagawa Archaeological Foundation.

Kanagawa Archaeological Foundation かながわ考古学財団. (2006). *Myojindai Site, Myojindai-Kita Site (Myojindai Iseki, Myojindai-Kita Iseki* 明神台遺跡・明神台北遺跡*)*. Kanagawa Archaeological Foundation Investigation Report かながわ考古学財団調査報告 192. Yokohama: Kanagawa Archaeological Foundation.

Kanagawa Archaeological Foundation かながわ考古学財団. (2009). *Bukkō Site (Bukkō Iseki* 仏向遺跡*)*. Kanagawa Archaeological Foundation Investigation Report かながわ考古学財団調査報告 244. Yokohama: Kanagawa Archaeological Foundation.

Kanagawa Archaeological Foundation かながわ考古学財団. (2012). *Bukkō Shell Midden, Bukkō Site, Bukkōcho Site (Bukkō Kaizuka, Bukkō Iseki, Bukkōcho Iseki* 仏向貝塚・仏向遺跡・仏向町遺跡*)*. Kanagawa Archaeological Foundation Investigation Report かながわ考古学財団調査報告 279. Yokohama: Kanagawa Archaeological Foundation.

Kanpukuji-Kita Site Excavation Team 観福寺北遺跡発掘調査団. (1997). *Kanpukuji-Kita Site Group, Sekikōchi Site Excavation Report (Kanpukuji-Kita Isekigun Sekikōchi Iseki Hakkutsu Chosa Hokokusho* 観福寺北遺跡群関耕地遺跡発掘調査報告書*)*. Yokohama: Kanpukuji-Kita Site Excavation Team.

Kōhoku New Town Buried Cultural Property Investigation Team 港北ニュータウン埋蔵文化財調査団. (1985). *Preliminary Report on the Sannomaru Site Investigation (Sannomaru Iseki Chosa Gaiho 三の丸遺跡調査概報)*. Report on the Excavation of Buried Cultural Properties in the Kōhoku New Town Area 港北ニュータウン地域内埋蔵文化財調査報告 6. Yokohama: Yokohama City Buried Cultural Property Investigation Committee.

Nasunahara Site Investigation Team なすな原遺跡調査会. (1984). *Nasunahara Site (Nasunahara Iseki なすな原遺跡)*. Tokyo: Nasunahara Site Investigation Association.

Nasunahara Site Investigation Team なすな原遺跡調査会. (1996). *Nasunahara Site (Nasunahara Iseki なすな原遺跡)*. Tokyo: Nasunahara Site Investigation Association.

Orimoto Nishihara Site Investigation Team 折本西原遺跡調査団. (1988). *Orimoto-Nishihara Site (Orimoto-Nishihara Iseki 折本西原遺跡)*. Yokohama: Orimoto Nishihara Site Investigation Team.

Seki, Toshihiko 関 俊彦 and Tasuhiko Omiwa 大三輪 竜彦. (1973). *Higashi-Kaniwa Site (Higashi-Kaniwa Iseki 東神庭遺跡)*. Tokyo: Azuma Publishing.

Seki, Toshihiko 関 俊彦 and Tasuhiko Omiwa 大三輪 竜彦. (1974). *Kaniwa Site (Kaniwa Iseki 神庭遺跡)*. Tokyo: Azuma Publishing.

Tokyo Metropolitan Archaeological Center 東京都埋蔵文化財センター. (1996). *Tama New Town Site (Tama Nyu Taun Iseki 多摩ニュータウン遺跡)*. Tokyo Metropolitan Archaeological Center Investigation Report 25. Tokyo: Tokyo Metropolitan Archaeological Center.

Tokyo Metropolitan Archaeological Center 東京都埋蔵文化財センター. (1998). *Tama New Town Site (Tama Nyu Taun Iseki 多摩ニュータウン遺跡)*. Tokyo Metropolitan Archaeological Center Investigation Report 57. Tokyo: Tokyo Metropolitan Archaeological Center.

Tonoyashiki Site Group C District Excavation Team 殿屋敷遺跡群C地区発掘調査団. (1985). *Tonoyashiki Site Group C District Excavation Report (Tonoyashiki Isekigun C-Chiku Hakkutsu Chosa Hokokusho 殿屋敷遺跡群C地区発掘調査報告書)*. Yokohama: Tamagawa Cultural Property Research Institute.

Tonoyashiki Site Group Excavation Team 殿屋敷遺跡発掘調査団. (1983). *Summary of the Tonoyashiki Site Group Excavation (Tonoyashiki Isekigun Hakkutsu Chosa Gaiyo 殿屋敷遺跡発掘調査概要)*. Yokohama: Tonoyashiki Site Group Excavation Team.

Wajima, Seiichi 和島 誠一. (1968). *Santonodai (三殿台)*. Yokohama: Santonodai Site Excavation Report Publication Association.

Yokohama City Board of Education 横浜市教育委員会. (1965). *Santonodai (三殿台)*. Yokohama: Yokohama City Board of Education.

References

Yokohama City Buried Cultural Property Center 横浜市埋蔵文化財センター. (1990). *Yamada-Otsuka Site (Yamada-Otsuka Iseki* 山田大塚遺跡*)*. Report on the Excavation of Buried Cultural Properties in the Kōhoku New Town Area 港北ニュータウン地域内埋蔵文化財調査報告 11. Yokohama: Yokohama City Buried Cultural Property Center.

Yokohama City Buried Cultural Property Investigation Committee 横浜市埋蔵文化財調査委員会. (1980). *Orimoto-Nishihara Site (Orimoto-Nishihara Iseki* 折本西原遺跡*)*. Yokohama: Yokohama City Buried Cultural Property Investigation Committee.

Yokohama City Buried Cultural Property Investigation Committee 横浜市埋蔵文化財調査委員会. (1988). *Terayato Site (Terayato Iseki* 寺谷戸遺跡*)*. Yokohama: Yokohama City Buried Cultural Property Investigation Committee.

Yokohama City Buried Cultural Property Investigation Committee 横浜市埋蔵文化財調査委員会. (1989). *Report on the Excavation of Kanpukuji-Kita Site and Nippa Shell Mound (Kanpukuji-Kita Iseki, Nippa Kaizuka Hakkutsu Chosa Hokoku* 観福寺北遺跡・新羽貝塚発掘調査報告*)*. Yokohama: Yokohama City Buried Cultural Property Investigation Committee.

Yokohama City Buried Cultural Property Investigation Committee 横浜市埋蔵文化財調査委員会. (1972). *Moritohara Site, Yokohama City Buried Cultural Property Investigation Report (Yokohamashi Maizo Bunkazai Chosa Hokokusho* 森戸原遺跡: 横浜市埋蔵文化財調査報告書*)*. Yokohama: Yokohama City Buried Cultural Property Investigation Committee.

Yokohama City Historical Foundation Buried Cultural Property Center 横浜市ふるさと歴史財団. (1991). *Otsuka Site: Excavation Report of Yayoi Period Moated Settlement Sites 1, Structures Section (Otsuka Iseki: Yayoi Jidai Kango Shurakuato no Hakkutsu Chosa Hokoku 1, Ikohen* 大塚遺跡: 弥生時代環壕集落跡の発掘調査報告1遺物編*)*. Report on the Excavation of Buried Cultural Properties in the Kōhoku New Town Area 港北ニュータウン地域内埋蔵文化財調査報告 12. Yokohama: Yokohama City Buried Cultural Property Center.

Yokohama City Historical Foundation Buried Cultural Property Center 横浜市ふるさと歴史財団. (1993). *Ushigayato Site, Keshogadai-Minami Site (Ushigayato Iseki, Keshogadai-Minami Iseki* 牛ヶ谷遺跡・華蔵台南遺跡*)*. Report on the Excavation of Buried Cultural Properties in the Kōhoku New Town Area 港北ニュータウン地域内埋蔵文化財調査報告 14. Yokohama: Yokohama City Historical Foundation Buried Cultural Property Center.

Yokohama City Historical Foundation Buried Cultural Property Center 横浜市ふるさと歴史財団. (1994). *Otsuka Site (Otsuka Iseki* 大塚遺跡*)*. Report on the Excavation of Buried Cultural Properties in the Kōhoku New Town Area 港北

ニュータウン地域内埋蔵文化財調査報告 15. Yokohama: Yokohama City Board of Education and Yokohama City Historical Foundation.

Yokohama City Historical Foundation Buried Cultural Property Center 横浜市ふるさと歴史財団. (1995). *Kawawa-Mukaihara Site, Haradeguchi Site (Kawawa-Mukaihara Iseki, Haradeguchi Iseki* 川和向原遺跡・原出口遺跡*)*. Report on the Excavation of Buried Cultural Properties in the Kōhoku New Town Area 港北ニュータウン地域内埋蔵文化財調査報告 19. Yokohama: Yokohama City Board of Education and Yokohama City Historical Foundation.

Yokohama City Historical Foundation Buried Cultural Property Center 横浜市ふるさと歴史財団. (1999). *Komaru Site (Komaru Iseki* 小丸遺跡*)*. Report on the Excavation of Buried Cultural Properties in the Kōhoku New Town Area 港北ニュータウン地域内埋蔵文化財調査報告 25. Yokohama: Yokohama City Board of Education.

Yokohama City Historical Foundation Buried Cultural Property Center 横浜市ふるさと歴史財団. (2001). *E5 Site (E5 Iseki E5* 遺跡*)*. Report on the Excavation of Buried Cultural Properties in the Kōhoku New Town Area 港北ニュータウン地域内埋蔵文化財調査報告 27. Yokohama: Yokohama City Board of Education.

Yokohama City Historical Foundation Buried Cultural Property Center 横浜市ふるさと歴史財団. (2002). *Hachimanyama Site (Hachimanyama Iseki* 八幡山遺跡*)*. Report on the Excavation of Buried Cultural Properties in the Kōhoku New Town Area 港北ニュータウン地域内埋蔵文化財調査報告 31. Yokohama: Yokohama City Board of Education and Yokohama City Historical Foundation.

Yokohama City Historical Foundation Buried Cultural Property Center 横浜市ふるさと歴史財団. (2003). *Shimaibata Site, Kawawa-Mukaihara Site (Shimaibata Iseki, Kawawa-Mukaihara Iseki* 四枚畑遺跡・川和向原遺跡*)*. Report on the Excavation of Buried Cultural Properties in the Kōhoku New Town Area 港北ニュータウン地域内埋蔵文化財調査報告 32. Yokohama: Yokohama City Board of Education.

Yokohama City Historical Foundation Buried Cultural Property Center 横浜市ふるさと歴史財団. (2004). *Tsunasakiyama Site (Tsunasakiyama Iseki* 綱崎山遺跡*)*. Report on the Excavation of Buried Cultural Properties in the Kōhoku New Town Area 港北ニュータウン地域内埋蔵文化財調査報告 36. Yokohama: Yokohama City Board of Education.

Yokohama City Historical Foundation Buried Cultural Property Center 横浜市ふるさと歴史財団. (2006). *Main Excavation Report of Myojindai Site A District (Myojindai Iseki A-Chiku Honhakkutsu Chosa Hokoku* 明神台遺跡A地区本発

掘調査報告). Yokohama: Urban Renaissance Agency Kanagawa Regional Office and Yokohama City Urban Development Coordination Bureau.

Yokohama City Historical Foundation Buried Cultural Property Center 横浜市ふるさと歴史財団. (2007). *Kitagawa Shell Midden (Kitagawa Kaizuka 北川貝塚)*. Report on the Excavation of Buried Cultural Properties in the Kōhoku New Town Area 港北ニュータウン地域内埋蔵文化財調査報告 39. Yokohama: Yokohama City Board of Education.

Yokohama City Historical Foundation Buried Cultural Property Center 横浜市ふるさと歴史財団. (2008). *Keshōdai Site (Keshōdai Iseki 華蔵台遺跡)* Volume 2. Report on the Excavation of Buried Cultural Properties in the Kōhoku New Town Area 港北ニュータウン地域内埋蔵文化財調査報告 41. Yokohama: Yokohama City Historical Foundation.

Yokohama City Historical Foundation Buried Cultural Property Center 横浜市ふるさと歴史財団. (2009). *Kitagawaomote-no-Ue Site (Kitagawaomote-no-Ue Iseki 北川表の上遺跡)*. Report on the Excavation of Buried Cultural Properties in the Kōhoku New Town Area 港北ニュータウン地域内埋蔵文化財調査報告 42. Yokohama: Yokohama City Historical Foundation.

Yokohama City Historical Foundation Buried Cultural Property Center 横浜市ふるさと歴史財団. (2011). *Oppara Site (Oppara Iseki 大原遺跡)*. Report on the Excavation of Buried Cultural Properties in the Kōhoku New Town Area 港北ニュータウン地域内埋蔵文化財調査報告 44. Yokohama: Yokohama City Board of Education.

Yokohama City Historical Foundation Buried Cultural Property Center 横浜市ふるさと歴史財団. (2014). *Gondappara Site (Gondappara Iseki 権田原遺跡)*. Report on the Excavation of Buried Cultural Properties in the Kōhoku New Town Area 港北ニュータウン地域内埋蔵文化財調査報告 47. Yokohama: Yokohama City Board of Education and Yokohama City Historical Foundation.

Yokohama City Historical Foundation Buried Cultural Property Center 横浜市ふるさと歴史財団. (2017). *Gondappara Site II (Gondappara Iseki 権田原遺跡2)*. Report on the Excavation of Buried Cultural Properties in the Kōhoku New Town Area 港北ニュータウン地域内埋蔵文化財調査報告 49. Yokohama: Yokohama City Board of Education and Yokohama City Historical Foundation.

Yokohama City Historical Foundation Buried Cultural Property Center 横浜市ふるさと歴史財団. (2019). *Okkoshi Site (Okkoshi Iseki 打越遺跡)*. Report on the Excavation of Buried Cultural Properties in the Kōhoku New Town Area 港北ニュータウン地域内埋蔵文化財調査報告 51. Yokohama: Yokohama City Board of Education.

Acknowledgments

This research project was funded by the Japan Foundation. With the support of the Japan Foundation's Short-term fellowship, I was able to immerse myself in data collection in and around Tōkyō during the summer of 2023. As a result, I was able to demonstrate the usefulness of ancient Japanese materials in the recent and frequently discussed archaeological trend of examining wealth disparities by analyzing house sizes. I would like to express my heartfelt gratitude to Rowan Flad and Erica Brindley for inviting me to write this Element.

Cambridge Elements

Ancient East Asia

Erica Fox Brindley
Pennsylvania State University
Erica Fox Brindley is Professor and Head in the Department of Asian Studies at Pennsylvania State University. She is the author of three books, co-editor of several volumes, and the recipient of the ACLS Ryskamp Fellowship and Humboldt Fellowship. Her research focuses on the history of the self, knowledge, music, and identity in ancient China, as well as on the history of the Yue/Viet cultures from southern China and Vietnam.

Rowan Kimon Flad
Harvard University
Rowan Kimon Flad is the John E. Hudson Professor of Archaeology in the Department of Anthropology at Harvard University. He has authored two books and over 50 articles, edited several volumes, and served as editor of Asian Perspectives. His archaeological research focuses on economic and ritual activity, interregional interaction, and technological and environmental change, in the late Neolithic and early Bronze Ages of the Sichuan Basin and the Upper Yellow River valley regions of China.

About the Series
Elements in Ancient East Asia contains multi-disciplinary contributions focusing on the history and culture of East Asia in ancient times. Its framework extends beyond anachronistic, nation-based conceptions of the past, following instead the contours of Asian sub-regions and their interconnections with each other. Within the series there are five thematic groups: 'Sources', which includes excavated texts and other new sources of data; 'Environments', exploring interaction zones of ancient East Asia and long-distance connections; 'Institutions', including the state and its military; 'People', including family, gender, class, and the individual and 'Ideas', concerning religion and philosophy, as well as the arts and sciences. The series presents the latest findings and strikingly new perspectives on the ancient world in East Asia.

Cambridge Elements

Ancient East Asia

Elements in the Series

Violence and the Rise of Centralized States in East Asia
Mark Edward Lewis

Bronze Age Maritime and Warrior Dynamics in Island East Asia
Mark Hudson

Medicine and Healing in Ancient East Asia: A View from Excavated Texts
Constance A. Cook

The Methods and Ethics of Researching Unprovenienced Artifacts from East Asia
Christopher J. Foster, Glenda Chao and Mercedes Valmisa

Reconstructing the Human Population History of East Asia through Ancient Genomics
E. Andrew Bennett, Yichen Liu and Qiaomei Fu

Archaeological Studies on Gender in Early East Asia
Mandy Jui-man Wu and Katheryn M. Linduff

Environmental Foundations to the Rise of Early Civilisations in China
Yijie Zhuang

Self and Body in Early East Asian Thought
Mark Edward Lewis

Institutions and Environment in Ancient Southern East Asia (3000 BCE to 300 CE)
Maxim Korolkov

Unearthing Fluctuating Wealth Inequality: Household Disparities at Jōmon and Yayoi Sites in Southern Kantō, Japan
Yoko Nishimura

A full series listing is available at: www.cambridge.org/EAEA

For EU product safety concerns, contact us at Calle de José Abascal, 56–1°, 28003 Madrid, Spain or eugpsr@cambridge.org.

www.ingramcontent.com/pod-product-compliance
Ingram Content Group UK Ltd.
Pitfield, Milton Keynes, MK11 3LW, UK
UKHW022320240426
470365UK00021B/717